THE
BRAIN EATER'S BIBLE

THE BRAIN EATER'S BIBLE. Copyright © 2010 by Mythodrome, Inc. All rights reserved. Printed in China. For information, address St. Martin's Press, 175 Fifth Avenue, New York, N.Y. 10010.

The Brain Eater's and logo are registered trademarks of Mythodrome, Inc.

www.stmartins.com

ISBN 978-1-250-02401-5 (trade paperback)

First published in the United States by Mythodrome, Inc.

First St. Martin's Griffin Edition: October 2012

10 9 8 7 6 5 4 3 2 1

THE BRAIN EATER'S BIBLE

PAT KILBANE
Writer, Creator, Executive Producer

BRIAN ULRICH
Lead Artist, Photos, Co-Executive Producer

DEAN JONES
Head of Makeup Effects, Co-Executive Producer

NEIL D'MONTE
Original Illustrations, Producer

BRIAN LAROSA
Casting Director, Movement Coach, Producer

OUR EXPERTS

Brandon Webb, Headmaster, U.S. Navy SEAL Sniper Course
Clifford Cates, Paramedic and Battalion Chief, Morrisville F.D.
Dr. Linda Zuckerman, PhD, Immunology
Dr. Evan Lessuk, Instructor, 5th Level, Tai Chi Chuan
Dr. Sohaib Kureshi, M.D., Neurological Surgeon
Victor Darby, Firearms Instructor, Oak Tree Gun Club

MAKEUP EFFECTS TEAM

Dean Jones, Kristy Horiuchi, Afton Adams, Maggie Dillon, Marina Gwynn, Ashley Hooker, Don Lanning, Kyle Morris, Justin Apone

WARDROBE

Rikki Techner, Maggie Dillon, Kristy Horiuchi

OUR ZOMBIES

Todd Wilkerson, Angel Pena, Stephanie Armstrong, Rochelle Robinson, Natalia Fedner, Chris Raiskup, Bill Blair, Will Barker, Lauren Stambaugh, Marina Gwynn, Kyle Morris, Alissa McGowan, Joanne McCallin, Brian LaRosa, Evan Lessuk, Adam Halbridge, Pat Kilbane

SPECIAL THANKS:
Niels Bonnevie (font design), Alex Lugo (additional illustrations), Mom & Dad, David Turner, John Monteith, Zeke Kamm, Dan Wilson, Oak Tree Gun Club, Melissa McQueen, Barney's Beanery, Rob Kirk, Valarie Barsky, Dave Bertelsbeck, Dow Thomas, Dr. Creep, Rick Overton, Abe Scheuermann, Matt Stevenson, David Connelly, Courtney Ulrich

THE
BRAIN EATER'S BIBLE

Sound Advice for the Newly Reanimated Zombie

by

J. D. McGhoul
with Pat Kilbane

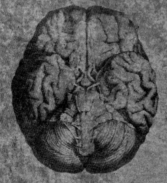

🦁 St. Martin's Griffin ≈ New York

CONTENTS

"I AM A ZOMBIE"

AUTHOR J.D. MCGHOUL

That's not an easy thing to say. I think the term is pejorative, really, since it implies a lack of intelligence, but I'm the last guy in the world to fight for political correctness. Let's just call it like it is. I'm a corpse, I walk around, I eat brains; I'm a zombie. Most zombies can't read, but, at risk of sounding elitist, this book is not for our plodding, dull-witted brethren. It is intended, rather, for the discerning undead, the rare few who have contracted this disease but remain insightful thinkers.

Waking up as a zombie is a troubling, disorienting experience. You still feel like yourself, yet you're untethered from reality by amnesia and possessed by a propensity to consume live human brains. These elements of "old self" and "new self" can be difficult to reconcile even for someone of above average intelligence. Further complicating matters is the new world into which you have awakened; filled with chaos, violence, and ill will, it is an unfit place to sort out your personal issues. Indeed, the deck may seem stacked against you, but have no fear. In <u>The Brain</u>

Eater's Bible, you and other zombies now have a powerful compass with which to navigate these treacherous waters. It is the culmination of my own relentless hunt for answers; the residue of deep contemplation, real world experience, and dutiful academic research. It contains excerpts from my personal journal, which I kept diligently from Day One, as well as photos, scientific illustrations, and other helpful found evidence.

I cannot emphasize enough the importance of educating yourself on zombie matters quickly and early. Failure to do so can leave you dead (permanently) before you even have the wherewithal to choose your path. This volume will be your key source of instruction. It will first orient you by exploring your brain-eating compulsions, as well as your physical origins and zombie anatomy. It will then move into practical concerns such as improving your man hunting skills, understanding your human enemy, and insuring you have a lengthy post-mortem existence. Finally, it will provide critical strategic information on winning the war against those who would destroy you. Long-term survival and contentment for our kind don't happen by accident; they are the result of deliberate lifestyle choices. So, for your consideration, I now share with you The Brain Eater's Bible, a collection of principles that lead to better undead living. Putting these teachings into practice will take time and discipline, but do so and the freshies will never know what hit them.

YOUR FIRST PIECE OF ZOMBIE ADVICE

IF THE SKIN ON YOUR HANDS IS BADLY SLOUGHING THE WAY MINE IS, YOU MIGHT WANT TO WEAR A LIBRARIAN'S RUBBER FINGERTIP OR A LATEX GLOVE TO HELP YOU TURN THE PAGES.

BEYOND THE HELP OF MOISTURIZER

JOURNAL ENTRIES

"MOUTHFUL OF MUD"

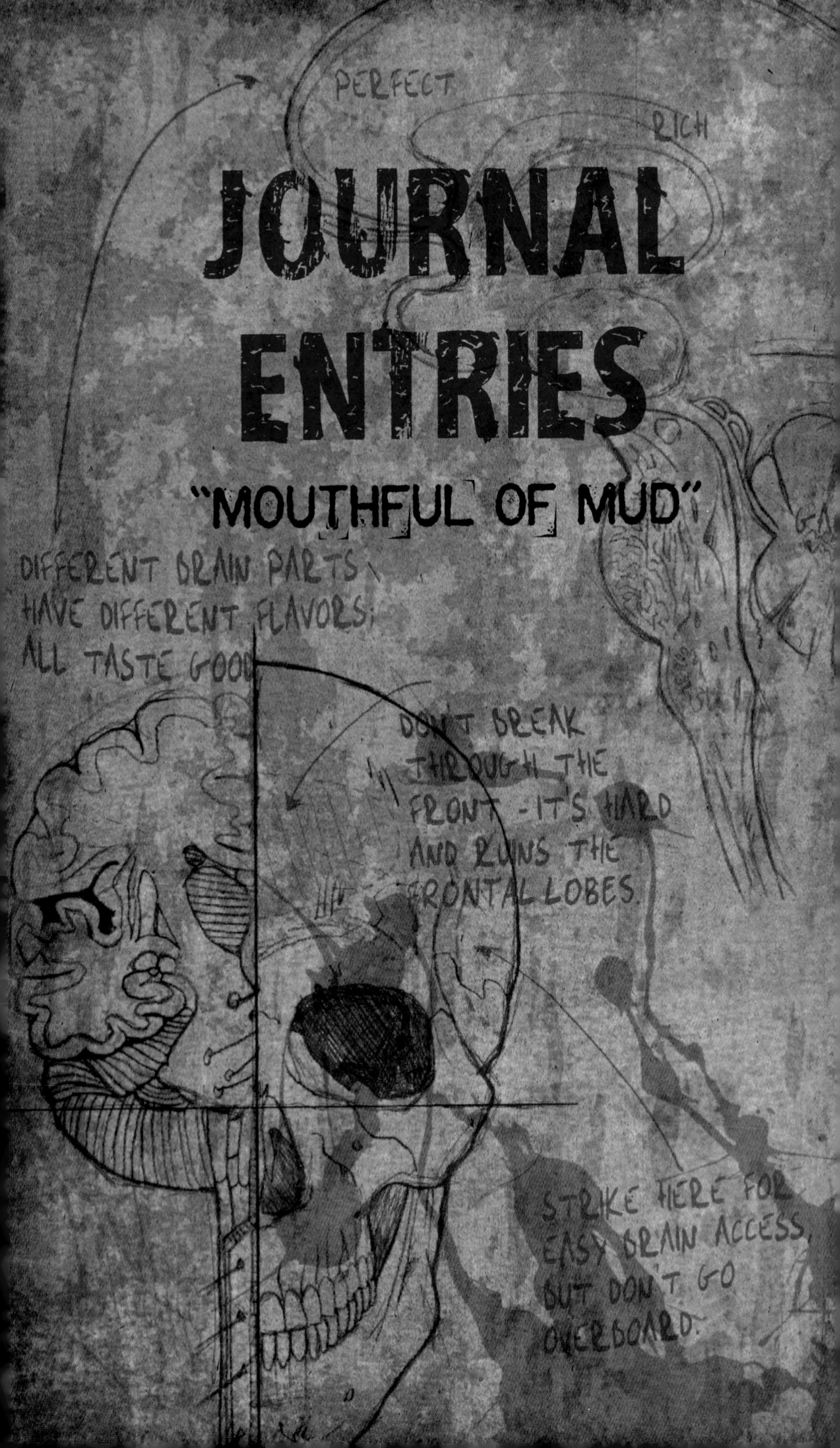

PERFECT

RICH

DIFFERENT BRAIN PARTS HAVE DIFFERENT FLAVORS, ALL TASTE GOOD

DON'T BREAK THROUGH THE FRONT - IT'S HARD AND RUINS THE FRONTAL LOBES.

STRIKE HERE FOR EASY BRAIN ACCESS, BUT DON'T GO OVERBOARD.

DAY ONE 6:35 PM
I'VE JUST DONE SOMETHING UNSPEAKABLE. I DON'T
KNOW WHAT OVERCAME ME, BUT I JUST KILLED AND
MUTILATED THREE PEOPLE AND FLED THE SCENE. THIS
CAN'T BE HAPPENING. I'M NOT CAPABLE OF MURDERING
THREE PEOPLE AND EATING THEIR BRAINS. MAYBE
THIS IS A REACTION TO PRESCRIPTION MEDICATION OR
SOMETHING, BECAUSE I WOULD NEVER DO WHAT I JUST DID.
THOUGHTS ARE COMING AT ME TWICE AS FAST AS I CAN
PROCESS THEM.

DAY ONE 6:47 PM
I'M NOT SURE IF I FEEL BETTER OR WORSE FOR HAVING
TAKEN A FEW MINUTES TO SETTLE DOWN. NOW THAT
I'M MORE RELAXED, THE REALITY OF THIS IS ALMOST
TOO MUCH TO TAKE. I'M AWARE THAT KEEPING THIS
JOURNAL IS GOING TO INCRIMINATE ME, BUT I DON'T
CARE. IF I DON'T GET MY THOUGHTS STRAIGHT I'M
GOING TO LOSE MY MIND. THIS IS WHAT I KNOW SO FAR:

MUCH OF MY MEMORY IS GONE, AND WHAT REMAINS IS
FUZZY. THE EARLIEST THING I CAN RECALL IS HAVING
A HORRIFYING NIGHTMARE - A DREAM THAT I WAS IN
COMPLETE DARKNESS AND UNABLE TO MOVE, AS SNAKISH
TENTACLES BURROWED INTO MY FLESH. I COULDN'T
BREATHE THROUGH MY NOSE AND COULDN'T COMMAND
MY MOUTH TO OPEN, WHICH LEFT ME HELPLESSLY
SUFFOCATING. THE PARASITIC ROPES GRIPPED ME AND
PENETRATED ME UNTIL I WAS ONE WITH THEM, TURNED
FOREVER INTO SOMETHING WRETCHED.

USUALLY WHEN YOU WAKE UP FROM A BAD DREAM,
THERE'S A SENSE OF RELIEF; YOU SEE THAT YOU'RE
ACTUALLY IN THE COMFORT OF YOUR OWN BED AND THAT
EVERYTHING'S FINE. NOT SO IN THIS CASE. WHEN I
FINALLY REGAINED CONTROL OF MY BODY AND JOLTED
TO CONSCIOUSNESS, HORROR GAVE WAY TO SHOCK AND
CONFUSION. I FOUND MYSELF FACE DOWN IN A FLOODED
DRAINAGE DITCH BY THE SIDE OF A FOUR-LANE ROAD,

CLUELESS AS TO HOW I GOT THERE. I WAS SO SHAKEN I TRIED TO CRY OUT, BUT MANAGED ONLY TO COUGH UP A LUNG-LOAD OF MUDDY WATER. THEN I NOTICED MY HANDS; THEY WERE PALE, DISCOLORED, AND PEPPERED WITH NASTY SORES. I QUICKLY REALIZED THE SAME SYMPTOMS WERE IN EVIDENCE ALL OVER MY BODY AND THAT I WAS IN DIRE NEED OF MEDICAL ATTENTION. I WAS GLAD IN THAT MOMENT I COULDN'T SEE MY FACE.

I NEXT RECALL FEELING A POWERFUL INSTINCT TO GRAB SOMEONE, WHICH WAS STRANGE GIVEN THAT THERE WASN'T ANYONE AROUND. I WANTED TO BEAR HUG SOMEONE TIGHTLY AND PUT MY FACE CLOSE TO THEIRS, BUT TO DO WHAT I HAD NO IDEA. AT THE TIME, I THOUGHT IT WAS JUST AN EXTREME NEED FOR COMFORTING, BUT EVENTS WOULD SOON PROVE THAT THEORY WRONG. I STRUGGLED TO MY FEET WITH A SENSE OF AIMLESS URGENCY, AND MY BODY STARTED WALKING. IT SEEMED TO KNOW WHAT IT WAS DOING, AND I JUST FOLLOWED ALONG. NONE OF THIS MADE ANY SENSE.

I STAGGERED ACROSS AN OVERGROWN FIELD TOWARD A SECOND-RATE STRIP MALL A FEW HUNDRED YARDS AWAY. THOUGH I COULD ONLY SEE IT FROM THE REAR, IT STRUCK ME AS BEING SOMEHOW FAMILIAR, STIRRING VAGUE MEMORIES OF A VIDEO STORE AND A LAUNDROMAT. I THOUGHT SURELY SOMEONE THERE WOULD LET ME BORROW A PHONE FOR AN EMERGENCY CALL. AS I WALKED, I CHECKED MY POCKETS FOR MY WALLET, FIGURING I WOULD PROBABLY NEED MY INSURANCE CARD, BUT NO LUCK. MY WALLET WAS GONE, AND IT SUDDENLY DAWNED ON ME I DIDN'T KNOW WHO I WAS. MY NAME, MY ADDRESS, FRIENDS, FAMILY - IT WAS ALL A BLANK. I WAS GROWING IRATE... AND HUNGRY. ARRIVING AT THE PAVED WALKWAY OF THE COMPLEX, I WAS RELIEVED TO FINALLY SEE OTHER PEOPLE, BUT THAT FEELING DIDN'T LAST. WHEN I MUTELY LOOKED TO THEM FOR HELP,

THEY SCREAMED AND MOVED IN THE OTHER DIRECTION AS QUICKLY AS POSSIBLE. I THOUGHT THEY WERE BEING A LITTLE OVERDRAMATIC UNTIL I CAUGHT A GLIMPSE OF MY REFLECTION IN A STORE WINDOW. HOLY JESUS. I LOOKED LIKE THE ASS END OF A ROTTEN PIZZA.

MY MIND WAS RACING; I THOUGHT, "I'M IN MEDICAL TROUBLE. I'M PROBABLY IN SHOCK. I DON'T KNOW WHO I AM OR HAVE ANY ID. PEOPLE DON'T WANT TO HELP." FINALLY, A MAN WITH A CONCERNED LOOK ON HIS FACE MOVED TOWARD ME, SAYING SOMETHING ABOUT HAVING EMT TRAINING. HE WOULD BE MY FIRST. AS SOON AS HE WAS CLOSE ENOUGH FOR ME TO REACH, I GRABBED HIM LIKE I'D BEEN WAITING MY WHOLE LIFE TO GRAB SOMEONE AND FINALLY DISCOVERED WHAT THAT URGE WAS ALL ABOUT. I OPENED MY MOUTH AS WIDE AS I COULD - SO WIDE MY JAW UNHINGED SLIGHTLY - AND TOOK A TALL, DEEP BITE OUT OF HIS NECK. BLOOD SHOT OUT OF THE WOUND LIKE A GEYSER AS THE POOR GUY SLUMPED TO THE SIDEWALK, HIS EYES LOCKED OPEN IN ICY FEAR. I THOUGHT, "WHAT THE HELL DID I JUST DO?!" THE ATTACK CAME AS A COMPLETE SURPRISE TO ME, SEEMING TO HAPPEN ON ITS OWN, LIKE A REFLEX PROGRAMMED BY A MILLION YEARS OF EVOLUTION. UNABLE TO HELP MYSELF, I GRABBED THE GUY AGAIN AND SMASHED HIS SKULL ON A PARKING BLOCK. IT WAS THEN THAT I GROANED OUT THE FIRST WORD OF MY NEW LIFE... "BRAAAINS!!!" AS I BEGAN SCOOPING UP PIECES OF HIS RUPTURED BRAIN AND STUFFING THEM INTO MY MOUTH, A WAVE OF ENERGY SURGED THROUGH MY BODY. IT WAS THE GREATEST PHYSICAL SENSATION I'VE EVER EXPERIENCED.

CHAPTER 1

EAT BRAINS

"The chief function of the body is to carry the brain around."

- Thomas A. Edison

A WAY OF LIFE

If you share my special problem, your need to eat brains will be self-evident. Your hunger for them will be compelling you in a way that no one could be prepared for, like a combination of all of your former human desires stacked on top of one another. Eating brains is not just a pastime, a form of nourishment, or a simple pleasure; it's your entire reason for being, obsessing you from the first moments of your new existence. Contemplative people so often struggle with what they are here for and what they should be doing with their lives, but for zombies these questions are already answered: you are here to eat brains. It's that simple. Your empty belly is the only void in your life that ever need be filled.

REASONS FOR EATING BRAINS

It's okay to eat brains without knowing exactly why. Bees don't intellectualize the honey-making process, and they do just fine. But in the interest of better understanding your worldly purpose, consider these important incentives for brain eating:

1) **Great Feeling** - Eating brains is an orgasmic experience, like devouring a fudge brownie sundae loaded with caffeine, steroids, and high self-esteem. One mouthful of lumpy cerebrum makes you feel immediately justified in your constant thoughts of feeding. And having an entire stomach full of brains? Forget about it. The sense of wholeness and empowerment it gives you is like nothing else. If the freshies had any idea how incredible it feels, they would willingly join the ranks of the infected.

2) **Physical Necessity** - I've never felt sick or weak as a result of insufficient brain intake, but going for too long without feeding does mess with your head. I tried abstaining from brains for a while once, and after about three days I started getting irritable. After a week I was impulsive and angry. Two weeks without brains rendered my typically clear thinking muddled and irrational, and three weeks brought me to the brink of insanity. I was explosively, unproductively violent and clinging to reality by a thread. The experience taught

SAY GOODBYE TO GREED

THERE WAS A TIME WHEN FINDING THIS BOX FULL OF CASH WOULD HAVE BEEN THE HIGHLIGHT OF MY LIFE. BUT MONEY AND ALL THE PLEASURES IT COULD BUY (BOOZE, WOMEN, FAST CARS) COULDN'T IN A MILLION YEARS EQUAL THE SATISFACTION I NOW GET FROM EATING BRAINS.

OVER EIGHTY-FIVE LARGE

me that if you choose not to eat brains, brain starvation will literally change your mind. You'll end up eating brains anyway, but not on your own terms; you'll be doing it recklessly and with the tortured mind of a madman. Whether or not this insanity can reach a "point of no return" I never want to discover.

3) Personal Improvement - Eating brains actually makes your body stronger without any tedious exercise (for biological details of the process see "Brain Gains" on pg. 46). The effect seems to be permanent, and cumulative to boot, which means that you've got a little more physical prowess every time you make a score. I once encountered a "slow mover" - a zombie who, unlike us, is physically and mentally slow - who had the strength of three men because of the amount of gray matter he had eaten. He didn't look like anything special, but it was a blast watching him knock down doors and tip over small cars to the amazement of his human quarry. Like so many slow movers, he was eventually destroyed by a lethal headshot, but I'm still inspired by what he proved was possible with real commitment to a diet of human brains.

SKINNY BUT STRONG - A SLOW MOVER I CALLED "BILL"

4) Bonding Experience - Everyone can use a friend, and you may travel long and far without meeting a zombie smart enough to carry on a proper conversation (the overwhelming majority of zombies are slow movers). Fortunately, you can still bond with your sluggish brothers and sisters through your shared interest in eating brains. Joining

slow movers on a hunt or satisfying feed can provide a sense of community, making you feel like you're a part of something bigger. Such is the unifying effect of brain eating; it creates a spiritual kinship that is palpable, even when unspoken. To use an analogy from your old life, if you ran into a guy who was a moron, you could always bond by talking sports. With zombies of any intellect - even none at all - you can always bond by eating brains.

5) Expression of Dominance - There is a tremendous sense of confidence and achievement that comes from eating a brain. Outside of the drug-like physiological effects, there is imparted a deep moment of self-knowledge - a feeling of mastery over your prey. The idea that a creature had plans to kill you, and that you're now consuming the very organ with which it made those plans, is a profound concept indeed. Harvesting a brain reminds you that you are good at something; that once again there has been a contest, and you are the winner.

6) Perfect Food - Human brains are a food that exists organically in nature. They have everything your body needs and taste perfect with no cooking, no seasoning, and no side dishes. What more could anyone ask? Well, it might be nice if you could grab lunch without having to dodge a fire axe, but you get my meaning.

ANOTHER FRESHIE GETS OWNED

ONLY LIVE BRAINS; ONLY HUMAN

I'm not sure why we need live human brains specifically, but that seems to be the case. Animal brains, for instance, contain absolutely nothing of value to a zombie. If you're going to eat a dog brain, you may as well be eating a handful of sand. It's like apples and oranges (both of which, incidentally, also eat like sand). As far as dead human brains go, they are worthless too. The tissue loses its positive effect when the cells die, which means the clock is ticking on a brain as soon as its owner expires.

Eating a live human brain is like plugging into a nuclear

CAT BRAIN

battery that powers and strengthens the zombie body. I don't know exactly how it works, but I believe the mechanism to be part biological and part something mystical - something heretofore undiscovered that perhaps only Eastern medicine could hope to explain.

Here is my own pet theory:

HORSE BRAIN

LOOKS DELICIOUS, BUT DON'T BE FOOLED

The frontal lobe area of the cerebral cortex is responsible for both higher cognitive functions, like planning and decision-making, and human characteristics, like personality and affect. This area also provides seventy percent of the benefit you get from eating a brain. The remainder of the organ is still tasty and nourishing, but doesn't hold a candle to the juicy frontal cortex. This leads me to believe that what charges the zombie system is consuming not just biomass, but something unique to human beings, like the soul or free will. The awesome power of people to ponder their options and choose between good and

SEAT OF THE SOUL

ARISTOTLE CONJECTURED THAT THE SOUL RESIDES IN THE HEART, AS DID THE ANCIENT EGYPTIANS, BUT I AGREE WITH DAVINCI AND DESCARTES IN THEIR BELIEF THAT THE SOUL IS IN THE BRAIN.

LEONARDO DAVINCI

RENÉ DESCARTES

evil may be an ethereal substance that zombies can digest and assimilate. I know this idea seems outlandish and "new age," but the brain's caloric value alone is not great enough to account for the massive amount of energy a zombie gets from eating it.

LISTEN TO YOUR CRAVINGS

The intensity of your craving for a food is an excellent measure of that food's importance to your body. Humming birds, for example, crave sugar because their high-speed metabolism requires so much of it. Lions get the most pleasure from eating meat because their bodies need an abundance of protein and fat. Specific appetites are part of nature's magnificent design, insuring the survival of each species. In other words, your craving for brains is there for a reason, and it must be respected.

Some might argue that, like vegetarians, zombies should override their dietary cravings with their moral convictions. Whether or not it is natural to be a strict vegetarian is the subject of wide debate, but the bottom line is that zombies have no such choice. Vegetarians can satisfy a meat craving with tofu-turkey, or "tofurkey," but "tofuman brains" would never cut it for a zombie. Live human brains are the only food that gives you sustenance, and to override that craving with high-minded philosophy would mean your undoing. To

Tofuman

Zombie Owned & Independent Since 1911

VEGETARIAN BRAINS

100% Meatless Gray Matter Entree

NET WT. 2 LB 14 OZ (46 oz)

SERVING SUGGESTION

VEGAN KEEP FROZEN

bring the point home, what do you think would happen if meat were the only food that humans could eat? The word "vegetarian" would not exist.

I encourage you to let go of your ambivalence. The sexual revolution of the 1960s was a reaction to the '50s-era guilt heaped onto something enjoyable, natural, and necessary for the continuity of life. There is a lesson in that for us. Eating brains is our biological directive, and we should guiltlessly enjoy it as we were intended to.

TYPES OF BRAINS

I'm jealous of all you newbies out there who have yet to sample the wide variety of brains on the world menu. You have some thrilling first-time experiences ahead of you! I hate to ruin any of the surprise by telling you what to look for, but this book is in part about survival, and knowing in advance what brains are best for you may give you the survivor's edge. Below are the major categories of human brains as I understand them.

Child Brains
While a brain of any age is still edible, don't go out of your way for a child brain thinking it's going to taste "extra fresh." The majority of brain development in humans occurs before the age of eighteen, with the critical frontal cortex area being the last to fully form. As a result, the brain of a victim under eighteen will give you less benefit than that of an adult and will have an unripe, "green banana"

aftertaste. Also worth mentioning is that the human brain doesn't grow in a linear fashion, but in major spurts - one occurring in the first year-and-a-half of life, and another between the ages of twelve and seventeen. This means you should avoid brains under the age of twelve altogether since they are the worst in terms of their bitter taste.

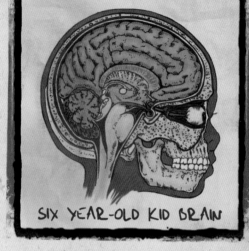

SIX YEAR-OLD KID BRAIN

Adult Brains

Between the ages of twenty and fifty, the human brain is in its prime and ready to reap. Unfortunately, this is also the age range when your prey will be at its physical peak. You'll have your work cut out for you making the kill, but the rush of eating a perfectly ripened brain will make it worth every ounce of effort.

Elderly Brains

The frontal cortex begins to atrophy after the age of fifty, so that eighty year-old, tottering geezer isn't the gravy train you thought he was. Degree of brain atrophy varies widely depending on genetics, lifestyle, and environmental factors, but as a rule, the brain of a senior citizen will be an inferior meal.

CATCH AND RELEASE

LETTING A FRESHIE KID GO FREE IS NOT A SELFLESS ACT OF MERCY; IT'S A MATTER OF PROPER HARVESTING. JUST LIKE A FISHERMAN WHO THROWS THE SMALL ONES BACK, THE IDEA IS TO GIVE THEM TIME TO GROW INTO A SUITABLE DINNER.

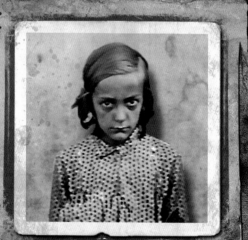

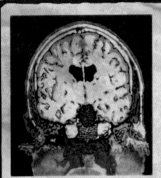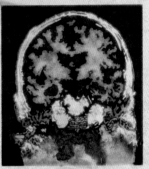

CT scans of a normal brain (left) and one ravaged by pugilistic dementia.

Damaged Brains

Any brain that has been chronically abused, like that of a boxer or drug addict, will be noticeably bland in terms of both enjoyment and revitalizing effect. As with elderly brains, this is a great example of getting what you pay for. If you see some guy shuffling down the street high on heroin and oblivious to threats, don't get too excited. He may be an easy score, but he's bruised fruit.

Big Brains vs. Small Brains

Where brains are concerned, size does matter, and bigger is usually better. The only problem is that you can't accurately determine the size of a brain by the size of the head that holds it. The skull contains many things in addition to the brain - all sorts of sensory organs, membranes, fluids, and cavities - and their proportions vary from person to person. For this reason, estimating brain size is always the roughest of guesswork until you've actually got the head cracked open and can take a look inside.

Smart Brains vs. Dumb Brains

There is a positive correlation between the intelligence of your prey and the nutritional value of the brain it possesses. As a guy who has eaten my share of scientists, though, I can tell you that geniuses aren't always good food. Some intellectuals have brains that are wired entirely for mathematics, resulting in bland, underdeveloped frontal lobes.

Mentally Ill Brains

I have precious little experience feeding on the brains of the mentally ill, with the exception of a known psychopath I felled recently. He was so-so eating.

Zombie Brains

In a moment of extreme hunger, the thought of eating a zombie brain may cross your mind (after all, we still look

TRUST YOUR GUT

YOU'LL FIND YOU'RE NOT COMPELLED AS MUCH BY BRAINS THAT DO YOU LESS GOOD. DON'T OVER-THINK THIS ONE WHEN ON THE HUNT; YOUR SENSES WILL NEVER STEER YOU WRONG.

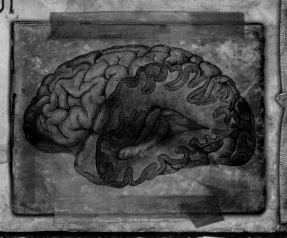

kind of human). All available information indicates that this would be a wasted effort. While I can't say for certain what the result would be since I've never tried it, we must have a zero-tolerance policy for this practice. Zombies have it hard enough in this world without turning on each other.

The Ideal Brain

This may be self-indulgent, but here's the brain/victim that I fantasize about when I'm hungry: a thirty year-old, sane, sober, healthy professor of philosophy, heavily involved in philanthropy and politics, with a wooden leg and an extreme disdain for firearms. I shouldn't tease myself by thinking about it.

A TOUGH NUT

If you're going to get at the brain, you first have to penetrate the skull, a rugged helmet of bone, and anybody who has ever tried to break one open knows how sturdy they are. The key to breaching the cranium is avoiding its convex and ridged areas, as these are structurally the stoutest. My favorite point of entry is the vulnerable "pterion" near the temple. A landmark of intersection between four cranial plates, the pterion is a structurally weak flat spot in addition to being the thinnest region of bone in the skull. It is so fragile, in fact, that even blows to the top of the head can cause the pterion to fail. Be careful when striking this area, though, because too much lobes, and you'll want to eat those intact (see "Brain Bits for the Connoisseur" below for nutritional details on the various brain parts).

This is where another great point of entry comes into play: the area below the nuchal line at the base of the skull. Since it is a "back way in," you can whack it much harder without harming the precious cortical tissue. You will have to clear some flesh away with your teeth first since this is an area of attachment for the neck muscles, but taking the time to do so has its rewards. A brain skillfully approached from below the nuchal line will have damage only to the cerebellum, leaving the entire cortex pristine for eating. So which area is the best way in? It all depends on how much time you have. If the work needs to be quick, use the pterion. If you have all the time in the world, go in through the base of the skull to preserve the frontal and temporal lobes.

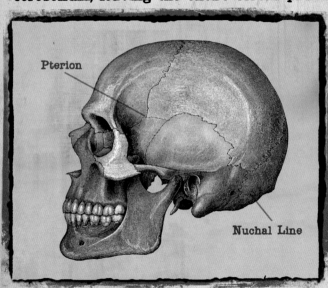

Pterion

Nuchal Line

Once you've chosen your spot, smash the cranium with whatever is nearby. For me that's usually a brick, a lamp, or something else handheld, but you could easily use the hood of a car, a cinder block wall, or even a public sculpture. Ideally, it will be something that also breaks the skin so you can get your fingers in there and pull the skull apart. As I mentioned previously, you can always clear away skin and muscle with your teeth, but <u>please</u> don't make the rookie mistake of trying to bite through a skull. I know how bad you want to get those brains in your mouth, but biting into solid bone will destroy your teeth, and they are the most critical weapon in your arsenal. The way I see it, you've already lost your looks. If you lose your bite too, you're going to be ugly <u>and</u> hungry.

A LESSON FROM THE WILD

TOOL-USING BLACKBIRD

I WOULD SAY THAT BITING THE SKULL BONE IS A BIRDBRAIN MOVE, BUT IT'S CLEARLY DUMBER THAN THAT. EVEN BIRDS HAVE THE GOOD SENSE TO USE TOOLS WHEN CRACKING THE HARD EXTERIOR OF THEIR PREY. EGYPTIAN VULTURES HURL STONES ONTO OSTRICH EGGS TO BREAK THEM; GULLS ARE KNOWN TO DROP SHELLFISH FROM A HEIGHT SO THEY SHATTER WHEN THEY HIT THE GROUND; AND COMMON BLACKBIRDS OPEN THE SHELLS OF SNAILS BY KNOCKING THEM AGAINST ROCKS.

BRAIN BITS FOR THE CONNOISSEUR

The brain, like a great lasagna, is a blend of complementary textures and flavors meant to be enjoyed together as a whole. This is fortunate since there is almost never time to extract and eat the parts of the brain individually. Circumstances generally call for you to swallow handfuls as fast as you can - first, to be sure you digest the brain while its tissues are still alive, and second, to affect an escape before the victim's angry buddy skewers your head with a pitchfork. For your edification, though, here is a gourmet guide to the various cuts of human brain, each rated from 1 to 10 for its nutritional value to zombies.

Brain Stem
Function: Control of involuntary processes, such as circulation, digestion, and breathing. Location: Extends from the spinal cord to the center of the brain. Trivia: Also referred to as the "reptilian brain" for its similarity to the crude thinking equipment of reptiles. Size Equivalent: A buffalo wing-sized chicken drumstick (1.5 oz.). Dining Notes: Composed mainly of white matter (axon strands covered with fatty myelin), the brain stem is lean and meaty; it is a simple pleasure whose primal origins will tease you with a

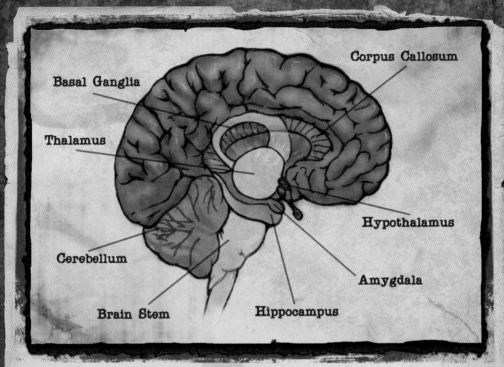

Basal Ganglia

Corpus Callosum

Thalamus

Cerebellum

Hypothalamus

Amygdala

Brain Stem

Hippocampus

suggestion of gaminess. To get the most out of a brain stem, you can suck on the top of the spinal column for a few extra morsels of meat. Nutritional Rating: 1

Cerebellum
Function: Vital to movement and balance. Location: Low rear of the brain. Trivia: Cerebellum is Latin for "little brain." Size Equivalent: A large lemon (4.8 oz.). Dining Notes: The cerebellum is the first area encountered when breaking out the base of the skull. It is made of gray matter (neurone cell bodies), so it is soft like thick custard with a flavor that is unsophisticated but always enjoyable. Nutritional Rating: 3

Thalamus
Function: Acts as a relay station between the brain stem and cerebral cortex. Location: Center of the brain. Trivia: Referred to as the brain's "sensory switchboard." Size Equivalent: Two unshelled walnuts stuck together (.9 oz. total). Dining Notes: A marvelous mid-meal treat, the thalamus has just the right serving size given its rich, pâté-like flavor. Nutritional Rating: 4

Hypothalamus
Function: Responsible for pleasure and motivational states. Location: Beneath the thalamus. Trivia: Lab rats given the

power to stimulate their hypothalamic reward centers will do so until they collapse. Size Equivalent: A cherry (.12 oz.). Dining Notes: The hypothalamus is almost identical to the thalamus in flavor and texture; in fact, you'll probably eat them together and not even realize they're separate organs. Nutritional Rating: 4

Basal Ganglia
Function: Regulatory mechanism for voluntary motor functions. Location: Lateral and above the thalamus in the brain's interior. Trivia: Parkinson's disease is the result of damage to the basal ganglia. Size Equivalent: Two small shrimp (.24 oz. each). Dining Notes: You'll encounter this pair of granular, spicy streaks after eating the cortex. Eat the brain from the side, as opposed to long-ways, if you want to best take advantage of the basal ganglia's wonderful flavor surprise. Nutritional Rating: 3

Hippocampus
Function: Critical to formation of new memories. Location: Straddling the upper brain stem. Trivia: Hippocampus means "sea horse." Size Equivalent: Two thick, uncut green beans (.5 oz. each) Dining Notes: These white matter tracts add a sweet, fleshy accent to the temporal area. Nutritional Rating: 3

Amygdala
Function: Operation of fear and aggression responses. Location: A few inches inside of each ear. Trivia: Name comes from the Greek word for "almond." Size Equivalent: Two almonds (.07 oz. each). Dining Notes: "I'll have the hippocampus with a side order of fear and rage." The amygdalae are dense, grainy morsels of gray matter that throw in exotic flair for the discerning brain lover. Nutritional Rating: 2

Corpus Callosum

Function: Connection of communication between the two cerebral hemispheres. **Location**: Beneath the longitudinal cerebral fissure separating the two halves of the brain. **Trivia**: Cutting the corpus callosum can result in "alien hand syndrome," where one of the patient's hands behaves independently, controlled unconsciously by its own side of the brain. **Size Equivalent**: Half a flattened bread stick (.5 oz.) **Dining Notes**: The corpus callosum is a nice, thick band of white matter that acts as a mellow sorbet. **Nutritional Rating**: 4

Cerebral Cortex - Frontal Lobes

Function: Essential for judgment, reasoning, and personality. **Location**: Behind the forehead. **Trivia**: This is the area of the brain destroyed by the lobotomy procedure performed frequently in the mid 20th century - a tragic waste of amazing food. **Size Equivalent**: Two half-pound, ground beef patties (8 oz. each).* **Dining Notes**: The frontal lobes are a true miracle food. Their gray matter has a thick custard texture, while the white matter beneath them melts in your mouth like cream cheese. It's heavenly, fatty goodness. The meat fat flavor has the intensity of bacon or breaded chicken skin, but without the greasiness. **Nutritional Rating**: 10

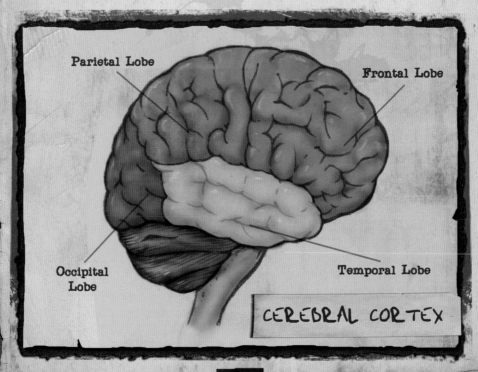

CEREBRAL CORTEX

Cerebral Cortex - Temporal Lobes

Function: Management of hearing, language, and memory retrieval. Location: Sides of the head just above the ears. Trivia: Lesions in the temporal lobes can cause an overemphasis on trivia. Size Equivalent: A pair of cooked, boneless rib steaks (4.3 oz. each).* Dining Notes: Providing additional ounces of always-delightful cortex, the temporal lobes are hearty in character without being pedestrian. Great comfort food. Nutritional Rating: 7

Cerebral Cortex - Parietal Lobes

Function: Handle sense of spatial orientation. Location: In the rounded area at the top-rear of the head. Trivia: A study of Albert Einstein's brain revealed that he had unusually large parietal lobes. Size Equivalent: Two small salmon steaks (3.8 oz. each).* Dining Notes: Like the frontal lobes, the parietal lobes are good and fatty without being gristly or greasy. Their flavor is also similar, though milder and more complex. Nutritional Rating: 5

Cerebral Cortex - Occipital Lobes

Function: Primary center of vision. Location: Base of the skull above the cerebellum. Trivia: Disorders of the occipital lobes can result in visual hallucinations. Size Equivalent: The end of a tip roast cut into two (3.6 oz. each).* Dining Notes: The occipital lobes have an ideal gray matter texture and light gentility of flavor, making them a perfect way to end your meal. Nutritional Rating: 5

> **THOUGHT FOR FOOD**
>
> THE FRONTAL LOBES OF THE CEREBRAL CORTEX ARE THE RICHEST AREA OF THE BRAIN FOR ZOMBIE NUTRITION, SO IF YOU'RE SHORT ON TIME, EAT THE FRONTAL LOBES FIRST.

* The sizes and weights given for the lobes of the cerebral cortex include their subcortical white matter.

HEALTH CONCERNS

When I realized that I would be eating human brains on a regular basis, my first concern was contracting "laughing disease." I remember reading in the Guinness Book of World

YOU CAN'T SAVE IT FOR LATER

THE BRAIN EATING EXPERIENCE IS SO INCREDIBLE YOU DON'T WANT IT TO END, BUT SADLY, THERE IS NO BRINGING ANY HOME IN A DOGGY BAG. BRAINS ARE A FOOD THAT SPOILS IN MINUTES DUE TO CELL DEATH, SO THEY ARE EITHER 100% FRESH OR COMPLETELY INEDIBLE. THERE IS NO IN BETWEEN. I KNOW THEY ARE SOMETIMES REFERRED TO AS "GRAY MATTER", BUT WHEN IT COMES TO BRAINS, FRESHNESS IS A BLACK AND WHITE ISSUE.

Records that laughing disease, or "kuru," is the rarest disease in the world and is caused by eating human brains. The symptoms begin with deteriorating motor control followed by wild mood swings, then incontinence, immobility, and death. Like mad cow disease, its root cause is a rogue nerve protein that reproduces uncontrollably and basically turns your brain into a sponge. I have never encountered a zombie who suffered from laughing disease and am guessing it's just not a problem for us. We're pretty robust organisms compared to people, so all of those buggy little difficulties we had as human beings are probably a thing of the past. Also along those lines, if you are eating a brain and encounter rubbery pieces among the normally soft meat, you're probably biting into a tumor. Spit it out if you want, or just swallow it; it doesn't matter. It won't nourish your body in any way, but it won't do you any harm either.

ON CANNIBALISM

The definition of the word "cannibal," according to Webster, is "one that eats the flesh of its own kind." As I will describe in Chapter 2, you and I are not fully human, so it could be argued that we are not technically cannibals. A more accurate term to describe a zombie dietarily would be "anthropophagous," meaning "feeding on human flesh."

Semantics aside, cannibalism has received an unjustly bad rap throughout history. For most people, the word conjures images of twisted criminals, like Ed Gein and Jeffrey Dahmer, but they are only a small part of the man-eating big picture. Most often, cannibalism is a matter of survival. In 1972 a plane full of Uruguayan rugby players crashed in the Andes Mountains, stranding the men for weeks without food. Those who made it out alive did so by eating the flesh of their dead friends. A group of American settlers known as "The Donner Party" ate dozens of their own to stay alive during their ill-fated journey from Illinois to California in 1846. And the beleaguered troops of Napoleon Bonaparte cheated death by eating human meat during their wintry march home from Moscow. You'll notice that common among these stories, in addition to survival under extreme conditions, is the practice of cannibalism by respectable people: athletes, pioneers, and soldiers of First World armies. When it is a necessity, man-eating is nothing to be ashamed of.

CANNIBALS BASTE A HUMAN HEAD

In some human cultures, cannibalism was not even a matter of dire straits, but of pure practicality. Native tribes of Easter Island and the Congo regularly ate human flesh for nourishment because of a paucity of meat-bearing mammals in their environment. For them it was all about protein. In fact, cannibalism has been so consistently practiced over the course of Man's existence that people carry genes protecting them from diseases caused by eating human flesh. In my opinion, this is all evidence that man-eating is natural, and if people do it so frequently to subsist, then zombies are justified in doing the same.

THE PHORID FLY

WHEN IT COMES TO EATING BRAINS AND CREATING ZOMBIES, WE PACE VIRUS CARRIERS ARE NOT ALONE. THE SOUTH AMERICAN PHORID FLY DOES THESE SAME THINGS WHEN IT PREYS ON FIRE ANTS. IT USES A SYRINGE-

LIKE APPENDAGE TO INSERT ITS EGGS INTO THE BODY OF AN ANT, AND WHEN THE EGGS HATCH, THE NEWBORN LARVAE MIGRATE TO THE ANT'S BRAIN AND START CONSUMING IT. THIS CAUSES THE ANT TO BECOME A "ZOMBIE," WANDERING AIMLESSLY UNTIL THE LARVAE TURN INTO BABY FLIES. THE YOUNG FLIES THEN DECAPITATE THEIR HOST AND EMERGE FROM ITS HEAD FULLY EQUIPPED TO "INFECT" OTHER ANTS.

JUST LOVE IT

It's not enough to be compelled to eat brains; you need to love it. Ask any addict and you'll discover that there's a big difference between loving the drug and loving the addiction. For us it really needs to be both. Let yourself get into it. Become an expert. School yourself in every nuance of the process, like a fighter pilot who combines his killer instinct with arduous practice and academic study. Not only will you become good at it, you'll also find that the seemingly messy pursuit of eating brains is actually a beautiful and worthy art.

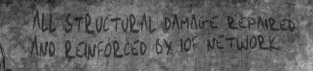

ALL STRUCTURAL DAMAGE REPAIRED
AND REINFORCED BY IOF NETWORK

JOURNAL

BROKEN SHOULDER

ENTRIES

"HELL'S RAGGED EDGE"

ELBOW BREAK

E-NODE IS VERY
SENSITIVE TO
PENETRATING
ATTACKS

SHATTERED SPINE

CHEWING SURFACES
ARE NO LONGER
NECESSARY.

INCISORS ARE
KEY FOR INFECTION

DAY ONE 6:47 PM (CONTINUED)
AFTER FINISHING MY BUSINESS WITH THE PARAMEDIC,
I BROUGHT MY VICTIM COUNT UP TO THREE BY
KILLING A MIDDLE-AGED COUPLE AS THEY CAME OUT
OF A SCRAPBOOKING STORE. I CAN'T GO INTO DETAIL
ABOUT THEM RIGHT NOW - IT'S JUST TOO AWFUL. TO
THEIR FAMILIES, THOUGH, I WANT YOU TO KNOW HOW
PROFOUNDLY SORRY I AM. I REALIZE THAT WHAT I DID
TO YOUR LOVED ONES IS SICK AND DISTURBING BEYOND
MEASURE.

WHILE WIPING THE COUPLE'S BLOOD AND BRAINS FROM
MY FACE, I FINALLY SNAPPED OUT OF MY FRENZY AND
STARTED SENSING I MIGHT BE IN DANGER. I THOUGHT
WITH ALL OF THE SCREAMING AND COMMOTION THAT
SOMEONE MUST HAVE CALLED 911, AND I WAS SO AMPED
UP I HAD NO IDEA HOW LONG AGO MY LITTLE RAMPAGE
STARTED. IT CROSSED MY MIND TO JUST WAIT FOR
THE POLICE AND TURN MYSELF IN - THAT WOULD BE THE
ONE SURE WAY TO END THIS WITHOUT ANYONE ELSE
GETTING HURT - BUT THAT IDEA WAS PRETTY SCARY
IN ITSELF. SURE, I'M A NICE GUY WITH THE BEST OF
INTENTIONS, BUT THEY WEREN'T GOING TO GIVE ME
PROBATION FOR MASS MURDER AND CANNIBALISM. IF
THE COPS DIDN'T SHOOT ME OUTRIGHT, AT A MINIMUM I
WAS GOING TO BE LOCKED UP FOR LIFE IN A MENTAL
INSTITUTION. I ENDED UP TAKING THE COWARD'S PATH.
WITH MY HUNGER SATISFIED, I DUCKED OFF BEHIND THE
SHOPPING COMPLEX AND SPRINTED SOME DISTANCE TO A
TREE LINE THAT LOOKED LIKE A GOOD PLACE TO HIDE.

THAT'S WHERE I AM PRESENTLY - CROUCHED IN THE
UNDERGROWTH, WRITING IN A NOTEBOOK I FOUND IN
AN ABANDONED SCHOOL BACKPACK. THIS LITTLE GULLY
AMONG THE TREES LOOKS LIKE A REGULAR HANGOUT
SPOT FOR SOME TEENAGE NE'ER-DO-WELLS, AND
THEY MUST HAVE SPLIT WHEN THEY SAW ME COMING.
THERE ARE TWO CIGARETTES ON THE GROUND STILL
BURNING, ALONG WITH DOZENS OF BUTTS, SODA CANS,

CANDY WRAPPERS, AND THE AFOREMENTIONED BACKPACK. ANYWAY, I'VE GOT A NOTEBOOK AND A PEN. I SHOULD ALSO MENTION I HAVE A FUNCTIONING WRISTWATCH ON MY ARM, AND HAVE SINCE I WOKE UP. IT'S THE GIANT KIND WITH THE LUMINOUS DIAL, TIME, DATE, STOPWATCH, AND EVERYTHING - WATERPROOF UP TO 300 FT. THESE WATCHES ARE WORN EXCLUSIVELY BY WORLD ADVENTURERS AND DOUCHEBAGS, AND THOUGH I'M NOT SURE WHICH I AM, I'M COMFORTED TO AT LEAST KNOW THE TIME.

DAY ONE 7:50 PM
THE SUN IS GOING DOWN, WHICH MAKES ME FEEL SAFER, BUT I'M EXPERIENCING A TERRIBLE DESPERATION AT WHAT HAS HAPPENED TO MY FACE. EVEN IF I GET WELL AGAIN, I WILL NEVER LOOK THE SAME. IT MAKES ME THINK OF ALL OF THE BURN VICTIMS AND OTHER DISFIGURED PEOPLE WHO GO ON OPRAH TO TELL THEIR STORIES. THAT WILL BE ME FOR SURE, DRAWING STARES AS I WALK DOWN THE STREET.

SOMETHING INTERESTING... I'M NOW LOOKING IN THE DIRECTION OF THE STRIP MALL AND REALIZING THAT I RAN ABOUT SIX HUNDRED YARDS AT FULL SPEED TO GET HERE. I SHOULD HAVE BEEN PUKING AFTER A RUN LIKE THAT, BUT I DON'T EVEN REMEMBER BEING WINDED. WAIT... THIS CAN'T BE. I JUST NOTICED I'M NOT BREATHING RIGHT NOW. NOT AT ALL.

DAY ONE 8:00 PM
I FORCED AIR IN AND OUT OF MY LUNGS JUST TO ASSURE MYSELF THEY WERE OKAY, AND THEY SEEM FINE. I FURTHER EXPERIMENTED BY INHALING TO SEE HOW LONG I COULD HOLD MY BREATH AND GOT TO EIGHT MINUTES BEFORE GETTING BORED WITH IT. I'M PRETTY SURE A NAVY SEAL CAN HOLD HIS BREATH FOR THREE MINUTES. A DOLPHIN CAN HOLD IT FOR SEVEN. WHAT DOES THAT MAKE ME? MY FACULTIES OF REASON

STILL SEEM SOUND, BUT WHAT I AM EXPERIENCING
IS TOO UNREAL TO MATCH ANY EXPLANATION BUT
DELUSIONAL INSANITY. WHATEVER THE CASE, I'M
PRETTY SURE THAT I'VE DONE SOMETHING HORRIFIC
AND THAT THE POLICE WILL BE OUT IN FORCE LOOKING
FOR ME. MY BODY IS SO ENERGIZED RIGHT NOW, PART
OF ME THINKS, "LET 'EM COME."

DAY ONE 11:44 PM
I'VE BEEN RIVETED FOR THE LAST SEVERAL HOURS,
SITTING TIGHT, WAITING AND LISTENING. WHEN I
HEARD SIRENS I FIGURED THE NET WAS BEGINNING
TO CLOSE, BUT NOW I'M ALSO HEARING THE SOUNDS OF
CIVIL CHAOS - SCREAMING, GUNFIRE, HELICOPTERS, AND
SCREECHING TIRES. WHAT THE HELL IS GOING ON?
IS IT TERRORISM? IS IT A RIOT? THE SIRENS AND
HELICOPTERS MIGHT BE FOR ME, BUT WHAT'S WITH THE
GUNFIRE? THE LONGER IT GOES ON, THE MORE I THINK
SOMETHING BIG IS HAPPENING THAT IS DRAWING LAW
ENFORCEMENT OFF OF MY PATH. I CAN'T BE THIS LUCKY.
I SWEAR THAT IF SOMEHOW I ESCAPE PROSECUTION I
WILL VOLUNTEER AT ANIMAL SHELTERS AND OLD FOLKS
HOMES FOR THE REST OF MY LIFE TO PAY PENANCE.
I'M DYING TO KNOW WHAT'S UNFOLDING OUT THERE.

DAY TWO 2:30 AM
THE ACTION KEEPS HEATING UP. SINCE IT'S A MOONLESS
NIGHT AND THERE'S SO MUCH LOUD NOISE, I SHOULD BE
ABLE TO GET AROUND UNNOTICED. I'M GOING TO CHECK
IT OUT.

DAY TWO 4:50 AM
ALWAYS KEEPING TO THE SHADOWS, I METHODICALLY
WORKED MY WAY TOWARD A MAJOR INTERSECTION
AND GOT A LOOK AT THE COMMOTION. PEOPLE ARE
CLEARLY FLEEING THE CITY, JUMPING IN THEIR CARS
AND HAULING ASS IN THE DIRECTION OF THE FREEWAY.
THERE ARE ALSO THOSE WHO CAN'T FLEE BECAUSE

THEY ARE TOO BADLY WOUNDED. THESE PATHETIC
SOULS WALK THE STREETS IN AN APPARENT DAZE
TOGETHER IN GROUPS OF FIVE OR TEN, SOME OF THEM
SO GRAVELY INJURED I DON'T KNOW HOW THEY ARE
STILL ON THEIR FEET. WHATEVER IS HAPPENING, IT
IS TRAGIC AND ON A SCALE THAT THREATENS THE
AMERICAN WAY OF LIFE. SELFISHLY, THOUGH, I'M KIND OF
THANKFUL. NOTHING SHORT OF A HUGE CATASTROPHE
LIKE THIS COULD SAVE ME FROM PRISON AND MAYBE EVEN
THE ELECTRIC CHAIR.

DAY TWO 5:18 AM
AS I CONTINUE TO EXPLORE THE AREA, INSTINCT HAS
CARRIED ME TO A MEDICAL RESEARCH FACILITY A HALF-
MILE FROM WHERE I FIRST WOKE UP. THE BUILDING IS
A NEW CONSTRUCTION WITH LOTS OF HIGH-END BIOTECH
EQUIPMENT, BUT THE PLACE LOOKS LIKE A WAR ZONE
INSIDE. IT IS SMOKE-FILLED (WHICH DOESN'T SEEM TO
BOTHER MY THROAT OR EYES) WITH PAPERS AND
BROKEN LAB GEAR STREWN EVERYWHERE. HALF-A-
DOZEN DEAD RESEARCHERS ARE LYING AROUND, BLOODY,
SLUMPED OVER, AND MISSING THEIR BRAINS. DID I DO
THIS? I HAVE A STRONG INTUITION THAT I WORKED HERE.

DAY TWO 5:43 AM
MY EFFORT TO FIND OUT MY IDENTITY WAS THWARTED;
THE PERSONNEL OFFICE HAS BEEN COMPLETELY
DESTROYED BY FIRE, WHICH PREVENTED ME FROM
ACCESSING THE EMPLOYEE FILES. THOUGH MY
VOCABULARY IS INDICATIVE OF AN EDUCATION, THE
COVERALLS I'M WEARING SUGGEST THAT MY JOB
HERE WAS NOT VERY TECHNICAL. WAS I AN INTERN?
I HOPE I WASN'T JUST A WANNA-BE, TALKING "BIG
SCIENCE" WITH THE EGGHEADS AS I MOPPED THE FLOOR
AROUND THEIR FEET. MAYBE NONE OF THAT MATTERS
ANYMORE ANYWAY. WITH ALL OF THESE PAPERS AND
EVERYTHING, IT LOOKS LIKE THERE'S A LOT I CAN
LEARN HERE. I'M GOING TO START READING TO SEE
WHAT I CAN FIND OUT.

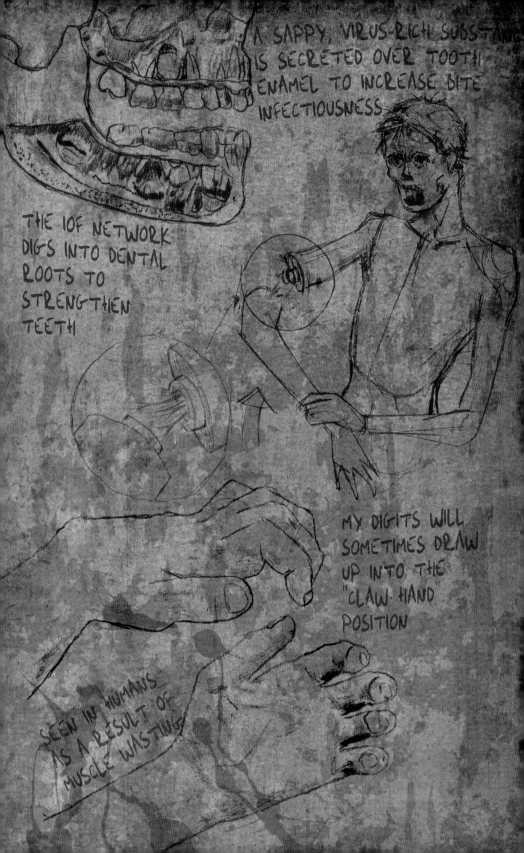

A SAPPY, VIRUS-RICH SUBSTANCE IS SECRETED OVER TOOTH ENAMEL TO INCREASE BITE INFECTIOUSNESS

THE IOF NETWORK DIGS INTO DENTAL ROOTS TO STRENGTHEN TEETH

MY DIGITS WILL SOMETIMES DRAW UP INTO THE "CLAW HAND" POSITION

SEEN IN HUMANS AS A RESULT OF MUSCLE WASTING

CHAPTER 2

KNOW YOUR BODY

"During those days men will seek death, but will not find it; they will long to die, but death will elude them."

- Revelation 9:6

A NEW YOU

Self-acceptance is a precondition of your being a high-functioning zombie, so before learning the business of how to hunt and kill, it's important that you first understand exactly what you have become. If you're not scientifically inclined, this chapter might be a little chewy, though, so hang tough.

THE PACE INFECTION

CLASSIC EXAMPLE OF PACE INFECTION SORES

The condition you are struggling with is known as Postmortem Ambulation with Cannibalistic Encephalophilia, or **PACE**. Born of controversial stem cell research, the **PACE** virus was created to undo the nerve damage caused by spinal cord injuries and actually succeeded in restoring movement to paralyzed limbs. Unfortunately, it is also highly contagious, 100% fatal, and turns the expired host's body into a sentient, undead, man killer. Oops.

A PLAGUE IS BORN

Human embryonic stem cells have the power to develop into any type of cell in the body; like college

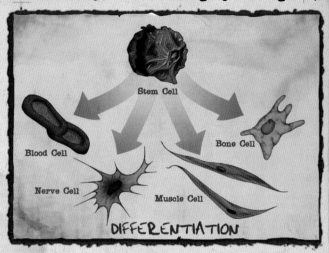

Stem Cell

Blood Cell

Bone Cell

Nerve Cell

Muscle Cell

DIFFERENTIATION

students who haven't yet declared a major, their options are wide open. Researchers thus saw in these "undifferentiated" cells the potential to become all-purpose building blocks, able to reconstitute nerve tissue and other body structures previously considered irreparable. But in addition to the scientific hurdles that stood in the way, there was a political battle over the ethics of sacrificing human embryos for medicine. Government funding came and went as the argument raged back and forth, forcing researchers to pursue new directions.

Instead of developing stem cell lines from embryos, biologists turned their efforts to "dedifferentiating" adult

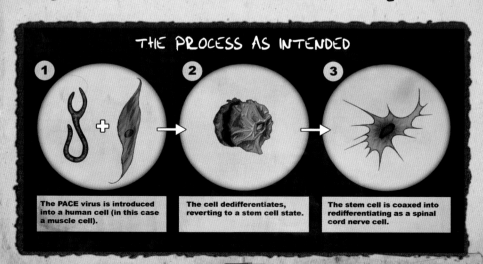

THE PROCESS AS INTENDED

1   2   3

The PACE virus is introduced into a human cell (in this case a muscle cell).

The cell dedifferentiates, reverting to a stem cell state.

The stem cell is coaxed into redifferentiating as a spinal cord nerve cell.

cells - transforming task-specific cells into cells that could become anything. Researchers would accomplish this with a man-made carrier virus, purpose-built to install a new strand of DNA within the human genome. The new DNA would effectively hit the "on" switch to the genome's dedifferentiating process, turning regular cells into stem cells.

The experiment was a huge success with human cells in the culture dish but produced no results in higher animal studies, so the biotech team did the unthinkable - they conducted illicit trials on live human beings. The side effects were apocalyptic in nature. Once inside a living person, PACE-infected cells manufactured more of the virus, spread it to neighboring cells, and then "burned out," dying

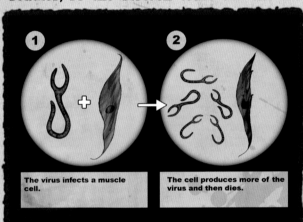

1

2

The virus infects a muscle cell.

The cell produces more of the virus and then dies.

by necrosis. The process repeated with an exponential progression, resulting in a wave of cell death that moved through the body at startling speed.

When the infection reached the brain stem, cells no longer died after replicating the virus; they instead dedifferentiated to a primordial state and redifferentiated

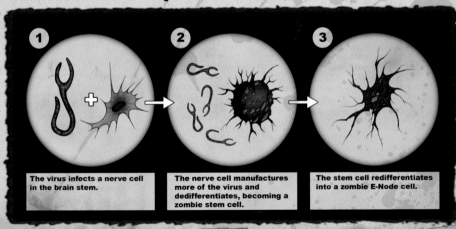

1

2

3

The virus infects a nerve cell in the brain stem.

The nerve cell manufactures more of the virus and dedifferentiates, becoming a zombie stem cell.

The stem cell redifferentiates into a zombie E-Node cell.

to form the structures and organs of a zombie. By the time the disease had run its course, a subject would be transformed from live human being, to cadaver, to reanimated flesh eater.

It's quite remarkable, really. What amazes me most is that the virus is just an "on" switch to the metamorphosis, so somewhere in the human genome the zombie blueprint must have already existed - an ancient, shadowy section of DNA coded for an entirely different creature. Where in the human family tree this DNA came from or what purpose it may have served is unknown. Some in the religious community might say that the strand is a "Doomsday Gene," bringing about The End Times and punishing mankind aptly for tinkering with creation. If this is true, you are more than a zombie; you are a horseman of pestilence and death.

INFECTION

Infection was a scary word in your old life, but you'll soon find it to have taken on new meaning; it now rolls off the tongue the way that "progress" or "victory" does. Fast-moving zombies owe their intellect and bodily speed to a most unusual means of infection, but it is too soon in your learning for me to share that with you now. The details of conventional infection are as follows:

THE PACE VIRUS

The PACE virus can only be transmitted by introduction through a break in the skin, usually from the bite of someone who is already infected. Scratches and other wounds caused by an infected host can also result in transmission, but the likelihood of it in those cases is not as certain. Once introduced beneath the skin, the virus attacks the nearest tissues and works its way through the body radially from the point of communication at a rate of about one inch per minute. This is an astronomical speed - about fifty times that of necrotizing fasciitis, the "flesh eating bacteria." Initial symptoms of PACE are typically similar to those of dry gangrene, beginning with aching and numbness in the afflicted area, followed by progressive discoloration. Skin ulcers then develop, and excruciating, mind-bending pain ensues when the infection reaches the torso. Eventually, when the advancing necrosis shuts down enough critical organs, the victim will die and lie motionless until the virus has completed its work. At that point the dormant host will be re-awakened as a zombie with a new, overpowering agenda: the consumption of live human brains.

Infecting The Dead

The virus <u>can</u> infect and reanimate people who are recently deceased, but only if it is introduced subcutaneously near the cranium within fifteen minutes after death (for more details, see "Encephalic Node" on pg. 37).

EXPIRED BRAINS: BITE OR NO BITE, THIS BODY WILL NOT BE GETTING UP

Infecting Animals

As the virus was developed for the human genome, it has no known effect on any other species. A pig, for example, bitten by a zombie, would itself become neither symptomatic nor infectious.

Amputation

When the virus is introduced into a victim's arm or leg, it is possible to stop the infection's march through the body by amputating the diseased limb. But this is much harder than it may seem in theory. The first problem is the speed at which the infection moves. If a person is bitten on the finger, for instance, in one or two minutes the bug will have spread to the meat of the hand, and three minutes after that it will have reached the forearm. This leaves a victim very little time to find the proper tools and mentally prepare for an amputation. The second problem is that amputation is both difficult and deeply uncomfortable. Human tendons and bones take work to saw

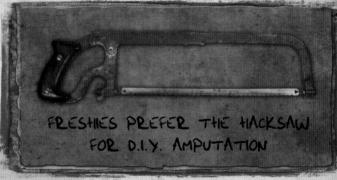

FRESHIES PREFER THE HACKSAW FOR D.I.Y. AMPUTATION

A FOLDING PRUNING SAW IS ALSO A GOOD EXPEDIENT

through, and if the pain of cutting major nerves makes someone pause for too long, the infection can overrun the site of the operation, forcing the already frazzled victim to try again farther up the limb with a fresh set of tissues and nerves. Every zombie's body tells a story, and the more of them you see, the better you'll be able to interpret their slashes, gashes, limps, lumps and holes. When you notice several deep, horizontal cuts on a zombie's limb, you're probably looking at the victim's failed attempts at amputation.

ZOMBIE ORGANS

Your new system of internal organs is primeval and coarse, but it is also extremely tough. It's almost as if nature has cut the Gordian knot and stripped us down to a set of rugged bare essentials. Though there is more to the zombie anatomy than I can describe here, these are the major points of interest:

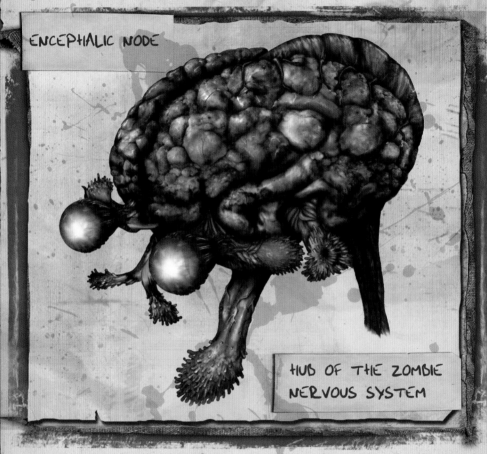

ENCEPHALIC NODE

HUB OF THE ZOMBIE NERVOUS SYSTEM

Encephalic Node

When the PACE virus reaches a victim's head, it converts the "reptilian brain" area at the base of the skull into zombie tissue, growing it into an "encephalic node," or "E-node," a gnarled ball of gristly nerve cells. This organ becomes the new center of thought for the undead being. Formation of a fully developed E-node takes about an hour and requires the presence of viable brain stem tissue, meaning the virus must reach the brain stem before too many cells have perished. When deprived of oxygen, cells in most parts of the human brain start dying after 4 to 6 minutes, but cells in the brain stem can survive quite a bit longer, buying the infection precious time to work its way there. As a rule, though, if a victim dies for any reason more than twenty minutes before the virus reaches the base of the skull, the amount of cell death will be too great for any possibility of reanimation.

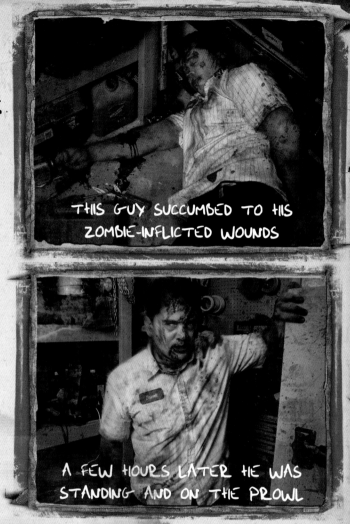

THIS GUY SUCCUMBED TO HIS ZOMBIE-INFLICTED WOUNDS

A FEW HOURS LATER HE WAS STANDING AND ON THE PROWL

The E-node is smaller and simpler than the human brain, with fewer of the squiggly "gyrations" that give mammal brains their macaroni-like texture. As of this writing, no detailed study of the E-node has yet been conducted to determine what sub-organs it contains or what their roles are in zombie behavior. What is known about the E-node is that, in addition to providing basic motor functions, it gives the average zombie the intelligence of an earthworm. This might seem like good news for the freshies, but earthworms are smarter than you think; they know how to eat, mate, flee from danger, line their burrows with leaves, and solve simple problems through trial and error. Underestimating the instinctive brainpower of slow-moving zombies has been the undoing of many a human being. (Needless to say, you and I are far brighter than earthworms, but again, the reason for this is information for a later chapter.)

Sensory Stalks
As the E-node approaches maturity, it builds thick bulbs of tissue toward the eyes, ears, nose, and mouth to provide mechanisms for the senses. I found little printed research on the subject of zombie senses, so I can speak only from my own experience here. My sight and hearing are comparable to what I recall in my pre-infection days, and my sense of smell is definitely more acute, but only where fresh brains are concerned. Funny story - someone once threw a Molotov cocktail at me and missed, and when it shattered on the ground, the wick was doused out before igniting the fuel. The stuff splashed all over my pants. I caught the guy and dispatched him, then realized while I was eating that I could smell the delicious brains but not the gas, or kerosene, or whatever it was on my clothes. My sense of taste is the same way. Brains give my taste buds (which are now on the roof of our mouths, incidentally) an intensely pleasurable sensation, while nothing else even registers. It's strange but also perfectly logical.

I have a suspicion that others among us may have different senses that are enhanced by PACE. I can't be sure, but some guys seem to be more visual or auditory hunters. Given that we often hunt in packs, this would give our species the maximum advantage when seeking human prey. It's possible that the E-node does a ping test on the host's existing sensory nervous system and builds to its strong suit (large ears or eye sockets, for example). Most of us are "sniffers," though.

UNDEAD PEEPERS

SOME ZOMBIES HAVE PUPILS AND IRISES, AND SOME ZOMBIES DON'T. THERE DOESN'T SEEM TO BE ANY RHYME OR REASON TO IT. I HAVEN'T PERCEIVED ANY CORRELATION BETWEEN EYE APPEARANCE AND VISION IN FAST MOVERS OR SLOW MOVERS.

Intraosteal Fiber Network

Once the E-node's development is complete, it extends tendrils down though the spine and into the skeletal system, constructing what is called the "intraosteal fiber network" or "IOF network." Fibrous tendons grow in and around the bones, replacing the need for muscle in giving the body power and movement. They also provide structural support, reinforcing broken bones, and allowing the host to stand and walk, even when the body is in a terrible state of repair.

The IOF network is also responsible for the reception of all tactile information, making your senses of touch and pain far different than they were in your pre-infection body. With your only mechanoreceptors now in your bones, every touch you perceive is a dull pressure, as if you were feeling it through thick layers of clothing. You probably wouldn't feel a finger tap on the shoulder, but you probably would feel a finger firmly poking you in the same spot. Basically, you've got all of the feeling you need to have essential

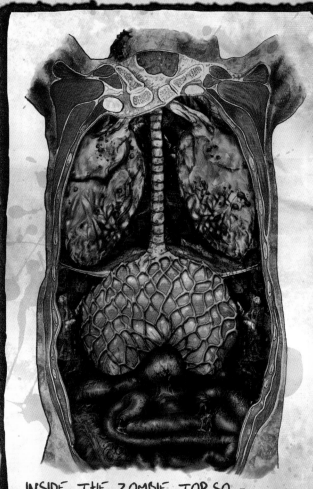

INSIDE THE ZOMBIE TORSO - VISIBLE ARE THE AIR BLADDERS, PREVERTEBRAL CONDUIT, GASTRIC SAC, AND VESTIGIAL ORGANS

body awareness, but no subtle sensitivity. As far as pain goes, there is none. Even a direct bullet hit to a bone - which is filled with zombie sensory fibers - will register only as a firm push. You have some sense of temperature as well, but it's also very muted; no physical discomfort results from even extreme heat or cold.

Unlike the E-node, the IOF network does not require viable tissue for its growth and development. The E-node is like a bulb from which the IOF network springs, and the network will grow equally strong and extensive independent of whether the flesh it permeates is alive or dead.

Prevertebral Conduit
As the IOF network's largest tendril creeps its way through the spinal column, a tubular structure called the "prevertebral conduit" grows parallel to it on the front side of the spine's exterior. This organ serves as both a zombie esophagus and wind pipe.

Air Bladders
The air bladders are simple, bilateral organs that emerge from the prevertebral conduit and fill the chest cavity, flattening the old lungs and pushing them to the rear. The zombie body doesn't require oxygen (for more on this see "Biochemical Needs" on pg. 47), so it appears that the only purpose of the air bladders is to pass air through the vocal cords, which are also crude, new structures. This allows for verbal communication ranging from groaning to

HUNTING/TRAVELING TIP

WALKING UNDERWATER IS A GREAT WAY TO GET AROUND UNNOTICED. IF YOU WANT TO MOVE ACROSS THE BOTTOM OF A LAKE OR RIVER, FLOOD YOUR AIR BLADDERS WITH WATER TO REDUCE YOUR BODY'S BOUYANCY.

articulate speech. Your new voice will be raspy, guttural, and never again what it once was. If you like singing, stick to Joe Cocker and Louis Armstrong.

Gastric Sac

The gastric sac is the zombie digestive system in its entirety, designed specifically for the processing of live human brains. Brains, once swallowed by a zombie, drop down the prevertebral conduit into this sturdy, stomach-like organ, located high in the abdominal cavity. There the material remains for a period of 3-4 hours while its life essence is absorbed. The gastric sac is typically about the size of two human brains but is incredibly elastic, stretching to hold as many as five adult brains at a time (that's fifteen pounds of brains!). Once the brains have been fully digested, all that remains of them are hard, clayish pellets that vary in diameter depending on the size of the pieces swallowed. They can be as large as a golf ball, or as small as a BB.

A PILE OF MY OWN WASTE PELLETS

At a time when the gastric sac is devoid of live tissue to digest, the pellets are regurgitated much the way a cat disgorges a fur ball, or an owl the skin and bones of its digested prey. Regurgitation will occur immediately if substances other than live human brain tissue are swallowed independently. The egestion process causes no discomfort, and will happen naturally and semi-voluntarily like a belch. Keep in mind that your waste pellets are an unmistakable sign to people that zombies are near, so hide them whenever possible if you are in hostile territory. You don't want to be tracked.

Vestigial Organs

The old organs of your host body serve little real purpose outside of giving you protection. The skeletal system does provide structural support, but the other tissues act primarily as soft body armor, absorbing the force of incoming blows and reducing the chances of your being killed or dismembered in combat.

BODILY CAPACITIES

Having already addressed the principal parts of the zombie body, we now turn to aspects of its performance.

Speed

Most zombies move at the pace of a slow walk, or about one mile per hour. This may seem unthreatenening until you consider that zombies never need to take a break. At that rate, in a single day they could pursue prey for twenty-four miles on foot, which is more than most human beings can manage. As one of the rare, fast-moving zombies, you can cover about fifteen miles of level ground in an hour, allowing you in some cases to even run down vehicle-mounted freshies.

SLOW ZOMBIES CAN COVER EIGHT MILES WHILE THE FRESHIES SLEEP

Strength

A zombie's strength has nothing to do with the muscle mass of his host body. Power in your limbs comes entirely from your IOF network. The deadly Bruce Lee was wiry but possessed incredible "tendon strength," and similarly, even rotten, gaunt-looking zombies can have deceptive killing power, all because of their thick, sinewy endoskeleton. In some ways, the process of "turning" is a great equalizer. Beefy body builders become zombies of average strength (or slightly higher, perhaps), while the handicapped become able-bodied, and the frail become far stronger than they ever were in human life. A typical zombie will begin his days with the strength of a pretty fit man, bench-pressing about 175 pounds.

Healing

Healing is an area where a zombie's appearance is deceptive - you do heal when you are wounded, it's just hard noticing it beneath your decrepit outer body. When there is damage to your organs and IOF network fibers, they are repaired extremely quickly. The fibers reach out to each other and re-weave themselves into place, which is especially valuable knowledge when it comes to amputations. If you get a limb hacked off in combat, grab it and get to safety as soon as you can. On both the stump and the limb you will see intraosteal fibers sticking out and wiggling like tiny worms. These are the strands that will affect the repair. Put the body part back in place and hold it there for at least ten seconds (the longer the amount of time, the better). When you let go, it will be reattached, but it won't

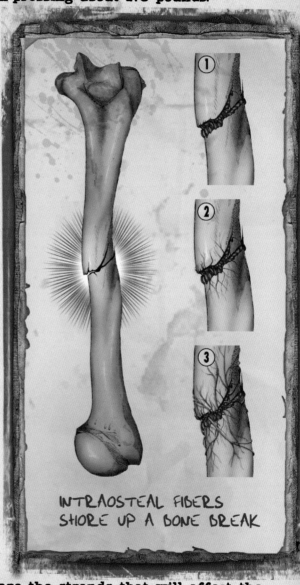

INTRAOSTEAL FIBERS
SHORE UP A BONE BREAK

be at full strength for another couple of hours, so don't push it too hard. This begs the question, "Can I attach another zombie's severed limb to my stump?" The answer is "yes." I know this only because it crossed my mind, and I tried it with my pinky toe. It worked like a charm.

If your air bladders get punctured you will find yourself unable to speak for a few minutes until the fibers on the edges of the wound get a hold of each other and create a weld. It's nothing to worry about. You'll be as good as new in a matter of hours. If your gastric sac is punctured, you may leak a little swallowed brains or waste pellets, but again, it will all be fine in a short time.

Sleep

That insomnia you're experiencing isn't stress; now that you're a zombie, you don't need to sleep and couldn't even if you wanted to. Physically, you don't even need to close your eyes. In fact, I'm convinced you could cut your eyelids off altogether and be fine with it. Psychologically, though, you may miss sleeping. Constant wakefulness - days, weeks, and months without interruption - requires a considerable mental adjustment. Your days will run together without sleep to separate them, and you will never have that feeling of a clean start that comes with waking up in the morning. The good news is that you never get

BURNING THE MIDNIGHT OIL

tired. People usually get fatigued after sixteen hours of being up, and anything beyond that brings on a miserable, frayed-at-the-edges feeling. With zombies, that just doesn't happen. You always feel sharp and ready as if you were perpetually at the peak of your day.

Reproduction

Zombies can no longer have intercourse (the male parts don't work anymore), but you can reproduce in a manner of

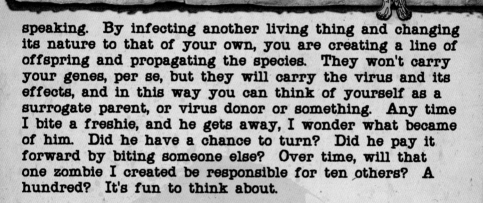

DON'T LOOK DOWN YOUR PANTS

IT'S A NORMAL REACTION OF CURIOSITY, ESPECIALLY FOR GUYS, TO WANT TO SEE WHAT THEIR GENITALS LOOK LIKE POST-INFECTION. TRUST ME WHEN I SAY THAT PEEKING IS NOT A GOOD IDEA. IF YOU THOUGHT A COLD SWIMMING POOL DID TERRIBLE THINGS TO YOUR MANHOOD, YOU DON'T WANT TO SEE THE WORK OF THE PACE VIRUS.

speaking. By infecting another living thing and changing its nature to that of your own, you are creating a line of offspring and propagating the species. They won't carry your genes, per se, but they will carry the virus and its effects, and in this way you can think of yourself as a surrogate parent, or virus donor or something. Any time I bite a freshie, and he gets away, I wonder what became of him. Did he have a chance to turn? Did he pay it forward by biting someone else? Over time, will that one zombie I created be responsible for ten others? A hundred? It's fun to think about.

OTHER ANATOMICAL FACTS

Here is a final handful of miscellaneous, but important, things you should understand about your body.

Brain Gains

As I mentioned in Chapter 1, eating brains doesn't just feel great; it fortifies your body. The most noticeable benefit, you'll find, is an increase in your physical strength. Every time you eat a brain, your intraosteal fibers grow more dense and powerful, even extending to the outside of the bones. From my estimates and personal experience, you get an increase in strength equal to about five additional pounds on your bench press for each healthy, adult brain you consume. As a defensive bonus, the intraosteal fibers within your skull thicken as well, making it more resistant to breakage and penetration, and better protection for your E-node (see "Permanent Death" on pg. 49). Once during a daylight prowl, I saw my reflection in the windshield of a derelict car and noticed I had a hand axe sticking out of my head. I had scrapped with some freshies the previous day and remembered feeling a good rap on my head while we were fighting, but I didn't give it another thought until I saw the axe. It looked ridiculous - like a Steve Martin prop - and I had been walking around like an idiot with it sticking out of my melon. I realized something important, though: had I not built up so much fibrous tissue on my skull walls from eating brains, that axe blow might have done a lot more than embarrass me - it might have killed me dead.

Biochemical Needs
Food (other than brains) and water are physically unnecessary for zombies to subsist. Zombies also have no need for oxygen in their biochemical processes, and that fact takes a little getting used to. To put it simply, you don't need to breathe. You might have an old knee-jerk reaction of panic when inhaling water or being shot in the chest, but it will pass. Exerting yourself indefinitely without getting fatigued is pretty amazing, as is swimming around underwater with no concern about when to surface.

Body Temperature
Unlike human beings, zombies are cold-blooded creatures. You can warm yourself somewhat with "microshivers" - tiny contractions of alternating intraosteal fibers - but for the most part, you take on the temperature of your surroundings. As far as your survival goes, the zombie body can function indefinitely in environments with

ME ON A COLD DAY'S HUNT

temperatures between -10°F and 120°F. At above or below this range, your E-node will eventually be destroyed by a breakdown of chemical compounds critical to its functioning. Be mindful that prolonged exposure to below-freezing temperatures, even when not a direct threat to your biochemistry, can freeze your vestigial tissues solid. When encountering these conditions, be sure to keep moving, periodically working all of your limbs over their full range of motion. Do this and you will crack the frozen flesh away from your joints and preserve your mobility; don't do it and you'll lock up like the tin man.

Decay
It may look rough, but your vestigial organic matter is not rotting. Cells killed by the PACE virus release potent toxins as by-products of their necrosis, rendering your dead flesh undesirable to other microbes. It is likewise of no interest to maggots, ants, rats, or other scavengers. If you were truly decaying, your body would bloat from the gasses released by the fungi and bacteria that were consuming it. Zombies do drip, stink, and change color, but this is the result of chemical changes in our tissue unrelated to decay. I know it may appear unattractive, so remember that your exterior of dilapidated skin, fat, and muscle is just the chaff of your former self. The real motor behind your functioning is the endo-network of fibers in and around your bones. You are elegant and powerful on the inside.

Dead or Alive?
After being described with expressions like "undead" and "living dead," you may be wondering whether you are technically dead or alive. The truth is pretty simple: your host body is dead, and you are alive inside it. Like a hermit crab that moves into a vacant snail shell, you are an organism that has taken up residence in the empty husk of a deceased creature. In your early stages of development, though, you were probably more analogous to a liver fluke, growing parasitically inside of a living host and draining its life away for your own benefit (not that there's anything wrong with that).

YOUR NATURAL LOOK

YOUR APPEARANCE IS THE RESULT OF YOUR PROCESS OF LIFE AS AN ORGANISM. YOU CAN'T BEAT YOURSELF UP ABOUT THAT. JUST TAKE A LOOK AT THE STAR-NOSED MOLE OR LEPTODES PIKE FISH, AND YOU'LL UNDERSTAND THAT BEAUTY IN NATURE IS ABOUT FORM FOLLOWING FUNCTION.

LEPTODES PIKE

Permanent Death

The one thing that is most likely to put you down for good is damage to your E-node. As indestructible as you may feel at times, your E-node is every bit as fragile as a freshie's brain when it comes to suffering a penetrating wound. It seems paradoxical, but it is critical to understand. An enemy can blow a gaping hole in the middle of your chest with a ten-gauge, and you'll spring back to your feet; but an ice pick stuck into your E-node can mean instant death, even though the wound is only an eighth of an inch in diameter.

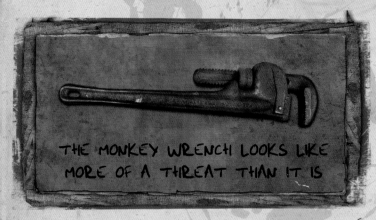

THE MONKEY WRENCH LOOKS LIKE MORE OF A THREAT THAN IT IS

In the case of blunt trauma to the head, there must be intrinsic physical damage to the E-node to have any real effect on a zombie. A moderate blunt blow to a freshie's skull can cause dazing, unconsciousness, or fatal edema, but a similar impact would only knock a zombie off balance. A blow to your head must carry enough power to crash through your cranium and directly disrupt your E-node if it's going to kill you.

Lifespan

I have no idea how long you can expect to live, but judging from the months I have been around and the strength and vitality of my body, I am guessing quite a while. Only time will tell us how it works - whether our systems gradually age, or perhaps suddenly burn out like a light bulb - so why not assume you'll be around for the long haul? The fact that we are tough, simple organisms makes me optimistic. Lobsters can live to be over 140 years old, and tortoises over 175.

1 M/S = 2.237 MPH

WORLD'S FASTEST MAN 22.4 MPH

JOURNAL

400 M RUNNER 19.5 MPH

ENTRIES

OLYMPIC SPRINTER

"BITTER AND RAW"

FAST MOVING

ZOMBIE

MPH

28
24
20
16
12
8
4

ZOMBIE BEGINS
TO GAIN

2 MIN   4 MIN   8 MIN   12 MIN

TIME RUNNING

ZOMBIE VISI
IS MOVEMEN
BASED FOR
HUNTING

POINT OF AIM
VS. POINT OF
IMPACT

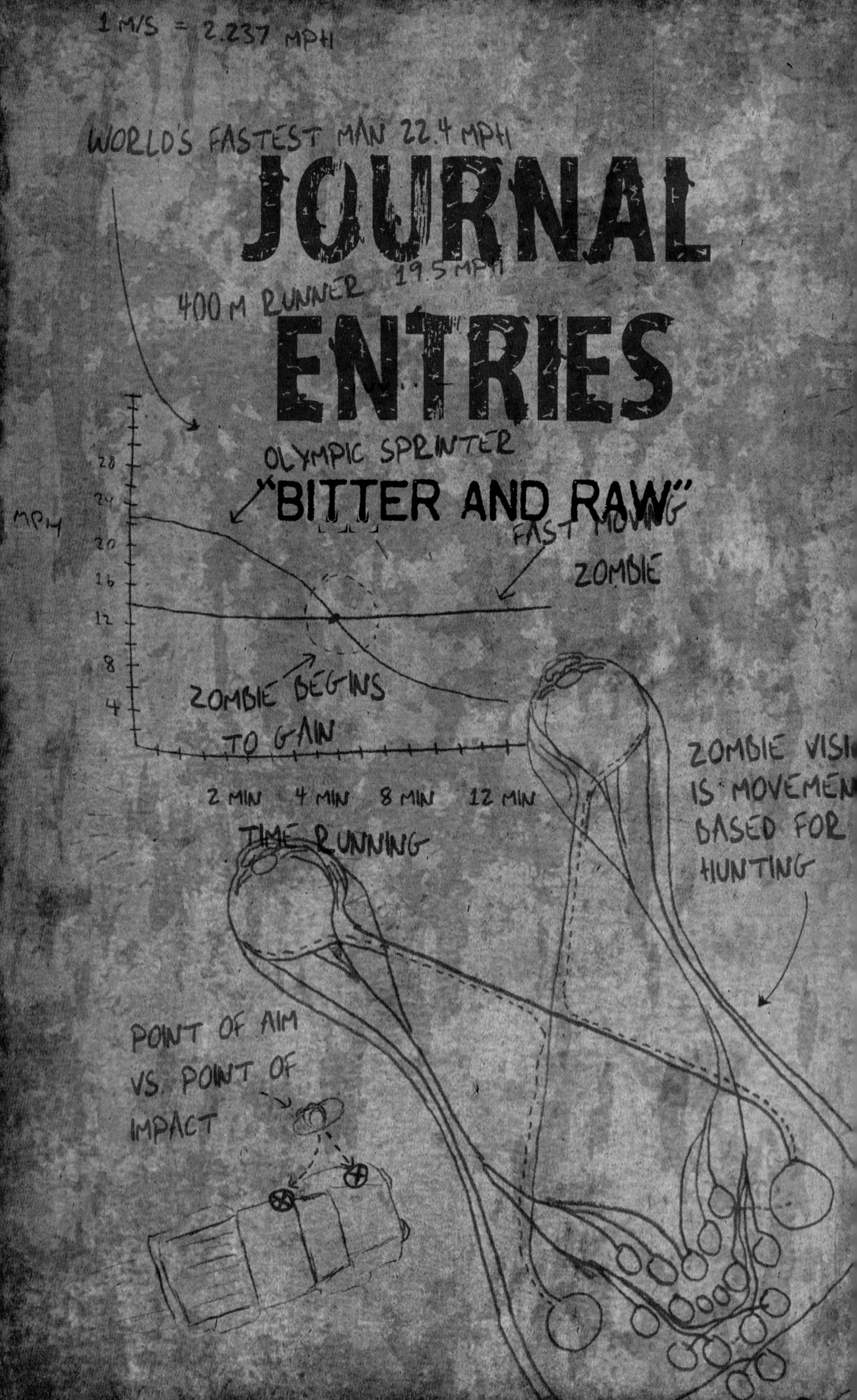

DAY TWO 2:40 PM

I'VE BEEN READING FOR OVER EIGHT HOURS NOW,
UTTERLY ENGROSSED IN THE UGLY TRUTH THAT
IS BEING REVEALED TO ME. LAB RESULTS, AUTOPSY
REPORTS, PRINTED CORRESPONDENCE - TOGETHER
THEY PAINT A CLEAR PICTURE OF WHAT HAPPENED. I
DON'T WANT TO BELIEVE IT. THE BEDLAM OUTSIDE IS
OBVIOUSLY THE VIRUS ON THE LOOSE, AND THE PEOPLE I
THOUGHT WERE THE WALKING WOUNDED ARE ACTUALLY
THE REANIMATED DEAD LOOKING FOR A MEAL OF
HUMAN BRAINS. NO AMOUNT OF WISHING WILL MAKE IT
OTHERWISE... I AM ONE OF THEM. BUT THE MATERIAL I'M
READING ONLY DESCRIBES MINDLESS ZOMBIES, SO I WONDER
IF MAYBE MY CASE ISN'T AS BAD. MAYBE FOR ME IT'S
EVEN REVERSIBLE. I NEED TO FIND OUT WHO DID THIS AND
MAKE THEM FIX IT, OR AT THE VERY LEAST MAKE THEM
PAY. I OVERTURNED A FILE BOX AND AM FILLING IT WITH
SELECTED DOCUMENTS FOR LATER STUDY IN CASE I NEED
TO CUT OUT OF HERE ON SHORT NOTICE; I TOSSED IN A
DIGITAL CAMERA FOR GOOD MEASURE.

I'VE SPENT A WHILE WANDERING AROUND THE PLACE.
THE BUILDING IS SINGLE-STORY WITH HIGH CEILINGS,
COVERING ABOUT SIX THOUSAND SQUARE FEET
ALTOGETHER. IT HAS TWO MAIN WORK AREAS: A
LARGER ONE FOR THE LAB EQUIPMENT AND A SMALLER
ONE FOR THE DISSECTION OF HUMAN TEST SUBJECTS.
THE LAB ROOM IS OUTFITTED WITH PCR MACHINES, DNA
SEQUENCING MACHINES, CENTRIFUGES, AND INCUBATORS,
AMONG OTHER THINGS. IT ALSO HAS A SUB-CHAMBER
RATED CL-3 (BIOCONTAINMENT LEVEL), WHICH I KNOW
DOESN'T COME CHEAP. THE AUTOPSY ROOM MOST
NOTABLY HAS FOUR STEEL TABLES, EACH HOLDING A
SPLAYED OPEN ZOMBIE. THE CREATURES HAVE MATTED
HAIR AND BAD TEETH, WHICH MAKES ME THINK THEY
WERE VAGRANTS, UNWITTINGLY "RECRUITED" FOR
EXPERIMENTATION. I IMAGINE THEM BEING LURED INTO
THE BUILDING WITH A SANDWICH AND GETTING A LOT
MORE THAN THEY BARGAINED FOR. THREE OF THEIR

BODIES WERE SAFELY DE-BRAINED, BUT ONE WAS NOT -
HE WAS DE-EVERYTHING-ELSED. ALIVE ON THE TABLE,
THE SMALL FOURTH ZOMBIE WAS STRIPPED OF ALL OF HIS
HUMAN BONES AND TISSUES, LEAVING ONLY HIS TWITCHING,
STRINGY, INNER NETWORK. AS I CROSSED THE ROOM,
HIS EYES TRACKED ALONG, PROTRUDING FROM HIS E-NODE
ON THICK, OCULAR STALKS. I KNEW FROM WHAT I'D READ
THAT HE WASN'T FEELING ANY PAIN, BUT THE SIGHT
WAS STILL TOO PATHETIC FOR ME TO BEAR, SO I PUT
HIM TO SLEEP BY SMASHING HIS HEAD WITH A TABLETOP
CENTRIFUGE. IT FELT LIKE THE RIGHT THING TO
DO. AS I WAS HEADING BACK OUT TOWARD THE LAB,
SOMETHING ELSE GRABBED MY ATTENTION - A TRIO OF
TOPPLED GURNEY BEDS WITH A COMBINATION OF METAL
AND NYLON RESTRAINTS. I STARED AT THEM FOR A
SOLID MINUTE. WHY WERE THEY SO COMPELLING TO ME?
THEY WERE EMPTY BUT HAD CLEARLY BEEN "SLEPT" IN,
MAKING ME THINK OF GOLDILOCKS AND HOW SHE WOULDN'T
WANT ANY PART OF THIS PLACE.

DAY TWO   4:45 PM
THE ENTIRE FACILITY LOOKS AS THOUGH AT LEAST
TWELVE PEOPLE WORKED HERE, AND THERE ARE ONLY
SIX DEAD RESEARCHERS, SO I'M BUSILY GOING THROUGH
THE LAB REPORTS AGAIN TO COMPILE A LIST OF
POSSIBLE SURVIVING STAFF. STAPLETON, WOLFF, SHULTE,
MCKENNA, FISHER, AND CATULLO ARE THE DEAD BODIES
(CONFIRMED WITH WALLETS AND SECURITY LAMINATES),
WHICH LEAVES THE FOLLOWING UNACCOUNTED FOR: MAY,
NOVAK, TAYLOR, REDLIN, AND ONE DR. MARTIN VERBEKE,
WHO WAS APPARENTLY IN CHARGE OF THIS HORROR
SHOW. I DON'T THINK ANY OF THE NAMES ON THE LIST
ARE MINE, BUT IT'S HARD TO TELL. IF I COULD TRACK
DOWN JUST ONE OF THESE GUYS, I MIGHT GET SOME
REAL ANSWERS.

I'M GOING TO SPEND ABOUT AN HOUR GATHERING A
FEW MORE THINGS AND TAKING ONE LAST LOOK AROUND,
THEN I'LL BUG OUT.

SON OF A BITCH. THAT WAS INTERESTING. I'M
NOW HIDING IN THE UTILITY HALL OF A FREE-STANDING
RETAIL BUILDING - IT LOOKS LIKE A PRINT SHOP OR COPY
CENTER OR SOMETHING. UNOCCUPIED, I HOPE. WHILE
AT THE LAB, I HEARD A RUSTLING NOISE COMING FROM
THE STOREROOM AREA AND WENT TO INVESTIGATE. I
WAS PRAYING IT WOULD BE ONE OF THOSE SADISTIC,
BASTARD SCIENTISTS, BUT WHEN I PEEKED THROUGH
THE OPEN DOORWAY, I SAW THAT IT WAS A CIVILIAN
WOMAN ROOTING THROUGH THE SUPPLY CABINETS. I
KNEW RIGHT AWAY SHE WAS INFECTED SINCE MY ATTACK
INSTINCT HADN'T BEEN TRIGGERED BY THE SMELL OF
BRAINS, AND SHE WAS COVERED WITH THE SAME SORES
I HAD. THE BLOOD AND BITS OF CEREBRUM SMEARED
AROUND HER MOUTH ALSO TOLD ME THAT SHE HAD BEEN
A BUSY GIRL. AS I WAS PIECING TOGETHER WHAT I
WAS SEEING, SHE SPOTTED ME AND MADE A BEELINE
FOR THE EMERGENCY EXIT. I COULDN'T LET HER GET
AWAY. IT WAS OBVIOUS SHE WASN'T A SLOW ZOMBIE,
BUT A QUICK, SMART ONE LIKE ME, AND THAT MEANT
WE COULD HELP EACH OTHER. I YELLED, "WAIT!" AND SHE
FROZE IN HER TRACKS HALFWAY OUT THE DOOR. IT
SOUNDS WEIRD TO SAY, BUT SHE WAS MY TYPE - KIND
OF A HIPPIE WITHOUT BEING FULL-BLOWN GRANOLA. IF
I HAD A FUNCTIONING HEART, IT WOULD HAVE SKIPPED
A BEAT. I TRIED EXPLAINING TO HER THAT I KNEW
WHAT WAS WRONG WITH US AND THAT I WAS GOING
TO LOOK FOR THE PEOPLE WHO WERE RESPONSIBLE, BUT
THE WORDS WEREN'T COMING EASILY. SHE STUDIED ME
FOR A FEW SECONDS AND FINALLY RESPONDED, "J.D.?" I
WAS DUMBFOUNDED. I THOUGHT "OH MY GOD, THAT'S MY
NAME! HOW DOES SHE KNOW MY NAME?" HER VOICE WAS
FROGGY AND STRANGE, BUT I LOVED IT.

THAT'S WHEN HER HEAD EXPLODED ALL OVER THE DOOR.
I ASSUMED IT WAS THE DISEASE THAT MADE IT HAPPEN
UNTIL I NOTICED THE BULLET HOLE IN THE DOORJAMB. I
NEVER HEARD THE GUNSHOT. IN A PANIC, I GRABBED

MY FILE BOX AND JOURNAL, AND RUSHED OUT THE WAY
I HAD COME IN - THROUGH THE FRONT ENTRANCE ON
THE OPPOSITE FACE OF THE BUILDING. I COULDN'T MAKE
MY LEGS MOVE FAST ENOUGH. AS I RAN DOWN THE
STREET, I LOOKED BACK OVER MY SHOULDER, CATCHING
A GLIMPSE OF THE GUY WHO DID IT; HE WAS A VISION
OF MENACE. ROLLING SILENTLY TOWARD THE LAB ON AN
ELECTRIC DIRT BIKE, HE WORE A CAMOUFLAGE BIOHAZARD
SUIT WITH HIS HIGH-POWERED RIFLE NOW SLUNG ON HIS
BACK. HE PANNED HIS HEAD METHODICALLY LEFT AND
RIGHT, BUT HIS EYES WERE HIDDEN BY THE SMOKED
LENSES OF HIS GAS MASK, SO I COULDN'T TELL IF HE SAW
ME OR NOT. IT SEEMS LIKE HE MUST HAVE, BUT EITHER
WAY HE DIDN'T GIVE CHASE. WHOEVER THE GUY IS, HE
DIDN'T BUY HIS EQUIPMENT AT THE LOCAL SPORTING
GOODS STORE. IT MAKES ME WONDER IF HE'S PART OF
A SPECIAL "CLEANING CREW" SENT BY THE ARMY AND
C.D.C. TO MOP UP THIS MESS.

THIS INCIDENT GAVE ME A LOT TO RUMINATE ON. I
THINK ABOUT HOW THAT GIRL'S FATE WOULD HAVE
BEEN MINE IF I HAD BEEN THE ONE TO WALK OUT THAT
DOOR. I ALSO THINK ABOUT HOW MUCH HOPE IT GAVE ME
TO ENCOUNTER ANOTHER PERSON WITH MY PROBLEM,
AND HOW MUCH LESS DESPERATE I WOULD HAVE FELT IF
SHE WERE WITH ME ON THIS HELLISH RIDE. FOR THE
MOMENT, THOUGH, THAT HOPE IS GONE, AND I FEEL A
HATRED SETTLING OVER ME FOR IT HAVING BEEN TAKEN
AWAY.

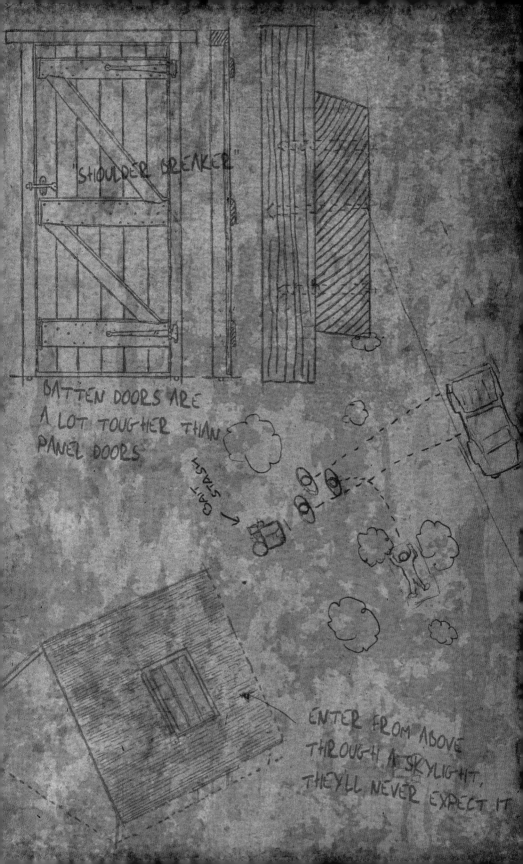

"SHOULDER BREAKER"

BATTEN DOORS ARE
A LOT TOUGHER THAN
PANEL DOORS

EXIT
START

ENTER FROM ABOVE
THROUGH A SKYLIGHT.
THEY'LL NEVER EXPECT IT

CHAPTER 3

HUNT

"A single death is a tragedy;
a million deaths is a statistic."

- Joseph Stalin

BRAIN ACQUISITION

Eating brains is your prime directive as a zombie, and your days of human consumerism are a thing of the past. Since you're no longer able to just "order in" or go shopping for food, you've got to get it the old-fashioned way - by catching it and killing it.

A SELF-PORTRAIT - GOOD TIMES IN A REST-AREA TOILET

OUR RIGHT TO MAKE PEOPLE EXTINCT

Zombies are hunting humans on a massive scale, which for some may raise moral questions about endangering homo sapiens as a species. Here are a few points you ought to consider: First of all, extinction for every species on earth is a simple matter of time. Even the fearsome dinosaurs that ruled the planet for millions of years eventually had to face an "extinction level event." Though human beings may seem special in their dominion over the earth, they are no different - just the next creatures in line to be wiped out. And we zombies happen to be their extinction level event.

Another argument for the unrestricted hunting of humans is that they are scientifically reckless and will eventually have to pay the price. When they detonated the first nuclear device, they did so believing that it might ignite the atmosphere and destroy the world. More recently, they built a miles-long particle accelerator that collided matter at such high speeds small black holes were forming. People can't keep doing that kind of thing and not have a problem sooner or later. If we stand down and let humans keep their planet, they will just end up destroying it with another ill-fated experiment.

Perhaps the greatest justification for man hunting is the vast number of natural species that people are rendering extinct. Human concern for other forms of life has been too small over the centuries for them to have earned our clemency. Keep in mind that zombies have no conflict with animals at all. You'll often see crows following packs of zombies, and I've shared my human kills with coyotes and wild dogs on several occasions. So what could be better for life on the planet - and the planet itself - than thinning the human herd? Harvesting down the human population will make Earth the blue-green Eden it was meant to be.

It's not lost on me that if human beings become extinct, our food source will be gone, but we'll have to cross that bridge when we come to it. For the time being, there's plenty to eat, and it's us or them. I can't be a proponent of conservation as long as there are still freshies shooting at my head. God only knows what the future holds; maybe we'll become extinct ourselves when we run out of food, or maybe we'll figure out some kind of brain farming or something. But if you trouble your mind looking that far down the road, you'll just lose focus and wind up in a bonfire pile with a screwdriver stuck in your noggin. First thing's first; hunt with extreme prejudice and quell the freshie threat.

PACK HUNTING

Slow-moving zombies roam by the thousands even in rural areas, so you'll always have the option of hunting with a pack. The bonding aspect of a group effort is nice, but practically speaking, there are advantages and disadvantages to the pack hunting approach.

LADIES NIGHT AT THE BRAIN BUFFET

Advantages of Pack Hunting:

1) Surrounding Prey - When with a group, you can encircle your quarry, cutting off possible directions of escape. Packs tend to descend on human-occupied structures from a single direction and then spread out evenly around them. With the freshies neatly trapped inside, you have some time to think about what your next move will be; and with hours or even days to ponder strategy, you can come up with some real gems. I once breached

a fortified mobile home by chaining it to a tractor and dragging it around until it fell apart. The slow movers were hobbling after me like kids following an ice cream truck.

2) **Physical Strength of Many** - The combined strength of the group allows them to tear through larger obstacles, like barricades and locked doors. You'd be surprised at the sturdy obstacles that will fall beneath the pressure of a hungry pack. What slow movers lack in I.Q. they make up for in determination.

3) **Spreading the Lead** - Defensively, you are in much less danger as part of pack since you are only one of many targets for a freshie with a gun. Being the only guy facing the fire sucks outright. You can go from hunter to hunted in no time flat.

BEST TO GET JUST ONE BULLET INSTEAD OF ALL SIX.

4) **Intimidation** - Large numbers of zombies induce panic in human prey, which often causes them to make poor tactical decisions. I remember one meek freshie actually throwing down his gun and surrendering when a mob of us burst into the room. Not a good choice. (For more on intimidation, see "The Human Fear Response" on pg. 105).

Disadvantages of Pack Hunting:

1) **Sacrificing Stealth** - Since zombies are instinct-driven creatures, your packmates can't keep themselves from moaning and wailing loudly when food is near. This blows the element of surprise, giving the freshies plenty of heads-up to flee or prepare for a fight. I should be over it by now, but it still annoys me when this happens.

2) **Less to Eat** - With a pack, you don't get as much to eat per individual kill made. Everyone is reaching in at once trying to get some brains, and there's no rhyme or reason to it. Being an orderly fellow, I wish they'd all get in line, but it's a zombie apocalypse, after all, not a

deli. On the bright side, brains fall apart pretty easily, so once a skull is opened, you're bound to get at least a piece in the ensuing frenzy.

3) Poor Team Coordination - Slow-moving zombies have no capacity for tactical thinking. More than a few times while pack hunting I've made a slick move to gain position, only to have my opportunity blown by a zombie who couldn't "read the game."

Pack Hunting Strategies:

If you do choose to hunt with a pack, you'll find that the increased number of variables makes it more complicated. At first, it will seem like quite a circus, but you'll eventually be able to anticipate the actions of your slow-moving teammates and start relishing the chess match. Here are a few tried and true approaches from my playbook:

1) Jumping the Runner - When your pack is closing in on a defended structure, get ahead of the group and take up a position by the building's rear exit. The groaning zombie horde sometimes causes people inside to lose their nerve and run, in which case you'll be perfectly situated to grab them when they squirt out the back.

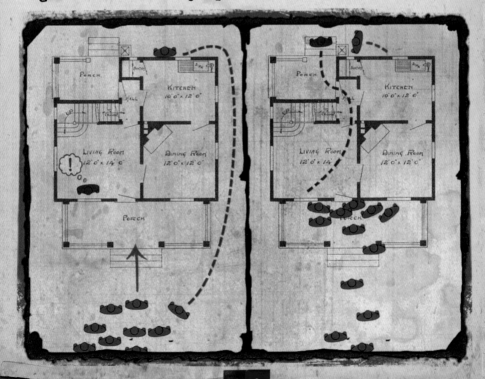

2) **Cat Burglar** - Wait until the pack has surrounded a structure and is pounding on the outside of it; then climb a trellis or drain pipe and sneak in a second floor window while the noisy siege is underway downstairs. Don't enter windows indiscriminately, though - get a look at who's in there first. I dove like a superstar through one window and had to dive right back out when I found the room full of pit bulls (four or five). They wouldn't have killed me, but they would have grabbed me and kept me busy until someone with a gun arrived.

3) **Fifth Man In** - Let the zombie pack do the heavy lifting in breaching the perimeter of the building, then follow behind at least four of them as you head inside. Those guys will take the bullets until you get close enough to surge to the front and finish the shooter. This isn't my favorite tactic since it sacrifices the lives of fellow zombies, but you may have to do it in a pinch. Your precious resource of reason is too valuable to put in danger for the sake of slow movers.

4) **Vehicle Ram** - Driving a vehicle through the wall of a freshie stronghold is a great way to breach it, but your slow packmates won't get out of the way for you. For

this reason, I've never been able to use a vehicle ram effectively in a siege (see "Don't Drive" on pg. 133 for more thoughts on vehicle use). On a related note, if outside of a defended structure you find an unoccupied vehicle with the keys still in the ignition, take them out and pocket them. Laying around somewhere I've got video footage of some pinkskins making a run for their car, only to discover the keys were no longer in it. This one guy does a panicked little dance as the pack envelops them. I've probably watched it a hundred times.

5) **Smoke Out** - If your pack has a freshie contingent holed up in an especially tough structure, lighting the place on fire can be a good way to get them out. You'll have to find fuel - gasoline siphoned from a vehicle, or tinder from a wooded area - as well as a way to ignite it. Starting the fire is tougher than you'd think since the lack of feeling in your fingertips makes matches and lighters hard to manage, but once the blaze is going, it will eventually drive your prey out. Make sure to cover all possible exits with fuel except one. This will guarantee that the freshies can escape the building and allow you to be waiting for them when they do. And no need to worry about the flames hurting your slow-moving zombie 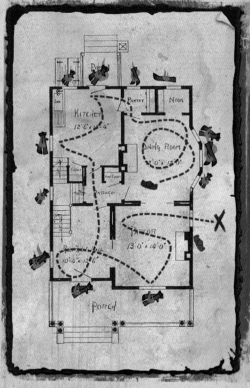 troops; they can sense the difference between heat that will singe their flesh and heat that will cook their E-node, and they will recoil from the latter.

6) **Slow, Slow, Quick** - This pack hunting tactic is the only one I recommend that isn't part of a building siege, but as with others above, it is deception-based. Most people have never seen a fast mover, and being around so many

slow zombies makes freshies complacent after a while. Just like a dumb driver who thinks he can beat a train across the tracks, people will sometimes get fancy with their judgment and cut it close. If you see a group of uninfected that is not well-armed, approach patiently with your slow-moving pack until you get to a point where you know you can close the gap, then break into a full sprint and watch the freshies shit themselves. When they scatter, pick a straggler, take him out with a speedy, violent attack, and assess from there whether it's worth going for a second kill. Remember, though, that your slow-moving friends will be right behind you, so grab your food and make a run for it unless you want to share with the rest of the class.

AMBUSH HUNTING

Ambush hunting can be extremely boring, but one of the bonuses of having PACE is that you don't need to eat, drink, or breathe to live, which means you can wait quite a while for prey to come along. You'll find a 3-5 day period is just a matter of patience, but your compulsion to feed will make it an act of extreme discipline to stay put for more than a week. Here are some techniques that I have found effective when hunting ambush-style:

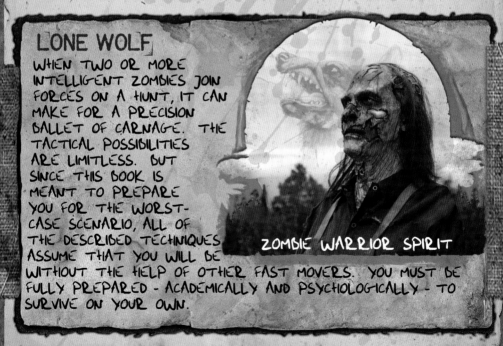

LONE WOLF

WHEN TWO OR MORE INTELLIGENT ZOMBIES JOIN FORCES ON A HUNT, IT CAN MAKE FOR A PRECISION BALLET OF CARNAGE. THE TACTICAL POSSIBILITIES ARE LIMITLESS. BUT SINCE THIS BOOK IS MEANT TO PREPARE YOU FOR THE WORST-CASE SCENARIO, ALL OF THE DESCRIBED TECHNIQUES ASSUME THAT YOU WILL BE WITHOUT THE HELP OF OTHER FAST MOVERS. YOU MUST BE FULLY PREPARED - ACADEMICALLY AND PSYCHOLOGICALLY - TO SURVIVE ON YOUR OWN.

ZOMBIE WARRIOR SPIRIT

1) **Supply Stakeout** - The key to being a good ambush hunter is knowing what the freshies need and where they go to get it. Anywhere there is food, clean water, or medical supplies is always a great place to start. My personal preference is the grocery store. Not expecting zombies to be smart, freshies will usually come right through front door and tactically "clear" the place like a bunch of police extras from Central Casting. Hide yourself inside the store somewhere near the front in a position where you can peek out and judge the group's size and strength. Be sure it's someplace they won't check, like on top of the frozen food coolers behind the signs and decorations. Next, wait until they are on their way out with armloads of provisions, because that's when they are the most vulnerable. At that point they think the hard part is over and are encumbered and preoccupied by the load they are carrying. As a bonus, they see the place as already cleared of threats, so they are not looking back when they leave as much as they are looking forward.

Watch for your moment and pounce on the last person out the door. Make your attack swift and gruesome. If you knock their head off or give them a blood-gushing bite to the neck, their friends will be stunned and will know immediately there's no point in attempting a rescue. Make a quick assessment of how tough the group looks. If they appear weak and rattled, go get yourself another kill. If they are drawing weapons, just drag the one you've got back in the store so they are more inclined to move along.

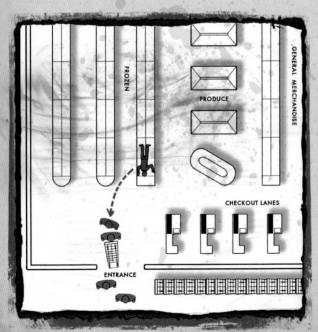

Hospitals and other large buildings are complicated to

use for ambushes since it's harder to predict where your victims are going to enter and exit. You can always watch from the roof to see where they come in, but it's easier just choosing a smaller location. If you want to use medical supplies as bait, go with a neighborhood clinic or pharmacy instead, and apply the same tactics. You'll find it much more manageable.

Notice I didn't mention gun stores on the list of good ambush spots. I've found these to be too risky. Some would argue it's a sound idea since the freshies you'll be facing must be low on ammo, but in my view, only the martially minded will risk their safety to gather firearms and ammunition, so you'll probably be in for a tougher fight in these places.

2) **Sexy Decoy -** Even in the midst of a zombie plague, human males respond predictably with their libidos. Here's something fun I tried that had a fair success rate. Get yourself a mannequin or other full-sized, posable female figure. I went to a porno store and found one of those $5,000 sex dolls that was especially life- like. Next, find 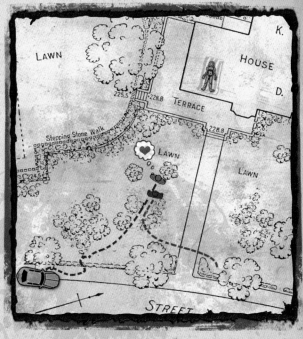 a structure located 75-100yds from the road that looks like a believable retreat for the freshies. Put the doll in skimpy clothing and pose it on the roof of the building to look like it's sunbathing or reading a book - something passive and seemingly human. Make sure to decorate the area with a chair, a towel, lotion, a cooler, or whatever makes the scene appear more organic. You won't have to wait long before some freshie guys drive past, park their car in cover, and creep out on foot to get a better look. Part of it is responsible reconnaissance, I guess, but most

of it is pure voyeurism and sexual desire. While they are distracted, make your way over to their position, get between them and their car, and engage.

3) Roadside Bait - Humans, especially here in the United States, are always trying to get something for nothing. You can capitalize on this foible by using material goods to bait them out of their cars. Place an empty 55-gallon drum and a jerry can about twenty yards off of the road in plain sight. If you want to really spice it up, lean an empty rifle against the fuel drum as well. Then dig yourself a shallow hide about ten yards off of the road and lateral to the line they'll be walking to get to the bait. Finally, camouflage yourself and wait for your prey to stop and investigate. When you hear someone get out of their vehicle and walk to the bait location, spring out and run at them at full speed. They will never expect it and will have almost no time to react. As a bonus, you'll now be in between them and their transportation, cutting off their escape, and any armed freshies still with the vehicle won't be able to shoot at you for fear of hitting their friends. Listen carefully before revealing yourself, though. If it sounds like there are four or more in the party, stay concealed and let them pass. Without knowing how well armed they are, you expose yourself to too much risk taking on more than three people in an outdoor battle.

4) Posing as a Freshie - I gave this a go early in my man-hunting career; I put on some clean clothes and a wig along with a latex Bill Clinton mask, and no one

ZOMBIE B.O.

I'M A BIG FAN OF FEBREZE. WITH ALL OF THE ICHOR AND BODILY HUMORS SEEPING INTO YOUR CLOTHES, SOMETIMES THE FRESHIES GET SPOOKED WHEN THEY SMELL YOU COMING. NEUTRALIZE THESE ODORS WITH A LITTLE SPRITZING, AND YOU'LL BE LESS NOTICEABLE TO THEIR NOSES.

DRIPPY = STINKY

was buying it even from a distance. Freshies are so paranoid of strangers that they will scrutinize you carefully before you can get close. They will see you're not walking right, if nothing else, and the jig will be up. It's embarrassing even talking about it, but for what it's worth, I've tried this little maneuver, and all it got me was two bullets in the chest.

NEW PRINCIPLES OF COMBAT

You are a far different animal now than you were in your pre-infection days, and you'll have to alter your combat thinking to suit your new capabilities. Continuing to think like a human may not get you killed right away, but it will certainly undermine your effectiveness. Consciously clear your mind of any old ideas you had about fighting and approach each situation with a fresh pair of eyes. You'll be amazed at what is now possible.

1) Beware of Human Fighting Systems - In theory, becoming a karate expert could help you in a tight spot, but you'll want to be careful about which moves you adopt. Designed for people, not zombies, human martial arts assume that combatants are subject to pain and injury all over their bodies. Wing-chun Kung Fu, for example, employs fighting stances that protect the groin from kicks, but who cares about that anymore? One time a guy gave me a full-on Scott Norwood field goal kick to the package, and to this day I laugh thinking about the look on his face when I didn't even flinch.

A FIGHTING STANCE USELESS TO ZOMBIES (AND MOST HUMANS)

With a zombie body you can now adopt a fighting style that is less about defense and more about inflicting damage.

2) Keep It Simple - I'm all for creative thinking, but don't get too fancy. To give you an example, I tried filling my air bladders with ammonia to cough it in people's faces when I got close, but even with practice, I found it helped too little to be worth the trouble. These kinds of methods are never as effective as your body's natural fighting tools, and too often they interfere with what you do best.

3) Wear Them Out - You don't develop an oxygen deficit when exerting yourself physically, so in any test of endurance with a freshie, you will be the victor 100% of the time. That means, whenever possible, you want to make them work their bodies; make them run from you, wrestle you, punch you - whatever suits the situation. They will lose strength by the moment and your advantage will mount.

One technique, which I call "The Run Down," employs this principle. If you are chasing human beings on foot, set your predatory instincts aside for a moment and use your zombie wits. The key here is not to catch them as quickly as you are able, but to keep the chase going for a while. Most freshies can only run at full speed for about one minute before becoming so gassed they are physically helpless, so close the gap to where you are about twenty yards behind them and maintain that spacing. You'll see when their body reaches its limit - their stride will become slow and irregular as they lose muscle control. That's when you take them down. They'll be so spent at that point, they'll have no answer for your attack. If you're going after

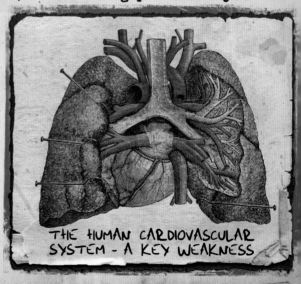

THE HUMAN CARDIOVASCULAR SYSTEM - A KEY WEAKNESS

a group that splits up, chase the smaller party. For
instance, if a group of three divides into a single runner
and a pair, take the single runner since he's the safest to
handle once you get a hold of him. Be careful, though,
the guy who heads off by himself is often the most
confident fighter. Also be mindful that a runner may
turn on you with a firearm, so in all cases be ready to
move evasively.

4) Watch and Wait -
Your sleeplessness
makes you able to
stalk humans more
effectively than
any predator in the
wild. If you spot
your prey and have
not yet been seen,
park your body and
sit still as a statue
until your opening
presents itself. I
once saw a lone
sentry standing
watch outside of a
boarded-up police

BIDING MY TIME IN THE ATTIC
UNTIL THE FRESHIES BED DOWN

station. He was bristling with weaponry (including a
.44 magnum), but something in his walk told me he was
tired. "Locking in" on him, I watched and waited for
my moment to come, and sure enough, he sat down and
started dozing. I killed him and dragged him off without
a sound. If you can, work every day on your mental
capacity to remain focused. Before you know it you'll
be able to lock in for an hour, then two, then four, then
eight. When you can sit and watch for that long, your
opportunity to strike with impunity will invariably come.
If you lose your patience and rush into a situation, it
might work for you once, but not ten times in a row, and
that's the kind of certainty you're looking for.

5) Abandon Fear - I don't know if you've ever seen those
nut-job Australian rules football players, but they
wear almost no safety equipment and hurl their bodies
into brutal collisions, seemingly without concern for
their health. Their all-out, aggressive style of play
overwhelms anyone who is not committing on the same

level. As I stated above, you can't be impetuous, but once you have decided to attack, you must have this fearless disposition.

One example of how I put this idea into practice is the "Bullet Man" technique. If you see one or two freshies escaping in a car, and you can reach it before it accelerates away, dive headfirst through a back-seat window whether it is rolled up or not. If it's rolled up, make sure to hit it with your head and not your arms, because your skull will definitely shatter the window, while your arms will not. Yes, the blow may break your neck, but such injuries are no longer of any concern to you. 100% commitment to this maneuver is a must, or it will be a laughable failure. Once through the window, pull yourself all the way into the car and begin attacking the person in the passenger seat. The driver still has to operate the vehicle, so he's not as much of a threat. When the passenger is incapacitated (dead or unconscious), focus your efforts on the driver. When he

OVERWHELM YOUR ENEMY WITH NAKED AGGRESSION

too is eighty-sixed, the car will likely be coming to a violent halt, so get low in the back seat and brace for impact. Don't do the Bullet Man if there are more than two people in the vehicle. You want one driver and one passenger (whom you will attack first). Two or more passengers will mean a free pair of freshie hands to put a steak knife through your eye socket.

CLOSE COMBAT ATTACK TECHNIQUES

Your battles will be many, and no two will ever be the same. Learning as you go, especially from the scary near misses, you will soon enough be a competent fighter. I encourage you to use your imagination in developing new techniques and creating a combat style that suits you. Here are some of the tricks that I have picked up in my travels:

1) Unarmed Foe Technique - If you want to make quick work of a squirmy, unarmed freshie, grab him in a tight bear hug and take a bite out of his face. This will make him turn his head away from you as far as possible, fully exposing his neck. Then you can literally go for the jugular (though the carotid is better). Bite away and his resistance will begin to wane immediately. Keep in mind, though, that the PACE infection moves lightning fast, so a face bite will start compromising your victim's brain tissue in less than five minutes. If you're going to eat, you'll have to do it right away.

2) Armed Foe Technique - In the case of an armed opponent, focus all of your attention on his weapon, whether it's a shotgun or a nail file. Grab the primary weapon arm with both hands and control it (in the case of a rifle you want to go for the trigger arm). Remember that in a scuffle, the muzzle of a gun can be pointing anywhere but at your head, so in general, you want to push the weapon downward. You can even stuff the muzzle into your chest or belly, causing your opponent to fire instinctively, wasting both his time and ammunition. Once your head is out of danger and

A FRESHIE'S WEAPON IS ALWAYS PRIORITY #1

you've got a hold of your enemy's arm, bite the hell out of it. Keep biting until he drops the weapon, and then transition to the "Unarmed Foe Technique".

3) Pre-Emptive Bite - Lay a bite on your opponent at the first safe opportunity, even if it's someplace seemingly ineffective. As soon as they are bitten, freshies know their lives are over, and it breaks their spirit. At this point, most will mentally clock out, becoming so shaken

UBER ZOMBIE

ONCE YOU'VE EATEN A HUNDRED OR MORE BRAINS, YOUR INCREASED PHYSICAL POWER WILL GIVE YOU GREATER LATITUDE IN YOUR FIGHTING STYLE. MEMBERS OF THE "CENTURY CLUB" CAN TINKER WITH THROWING PUNCHES, FOR INSTANCE, SINCE THEIR BLOWS WILL BE POTENT ENOUGH TO CAUSE IMMEDIATE UNCONSCIOUSNESS OR DEATH.

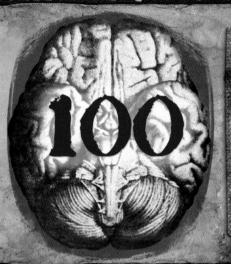

they are unable to fight strategically. Be aware that this technique can work against you; a freshie, once bitten, will sometimes get a burst of courage since he now has nothing to lose, but these cases are not common.

NOTE: The line between what is an attack and what is a defense can be a blurry one in the world of hand-to-hand combat, so it was not easy deciding which techniques should be included here and which belong in the defense-oriented pages of a later chapter. If you're looking for additional moves, there's a bevy of them under "Self-Defense Techniques" in Chapter 5.

USING FIREARMS

I suppose this is up to the individual zombie, but my instinctive advice would be to avoid using guns. Grabbing and biting is what you do best, and you can't grab your opponent when you have a gun in your hand. Ultimately, to have a firefight with a freshie is to do battle with his tools on his terms. Here's an example to illustrate my point: Let's say you enter a room and there's a freshie inside standing ten feet away with a pistol. If you rush him, you can close the distance in less than a second, giving him very little chance of putting a bullet in your E-node, especially considering that he will be panicked, and you will be moving erratically. Once you're on top of him, his weapon will be neutralized, and the fight will be all yours. On the other hand, if you have a gun and exchange fire with him, the shootout could drag on for as long as you both have ammunition. Yes, you can incapacitate him with hits to the body while he needs a head shot, but he will still get more rounds off than if you were to simply run right at him. How many chances do you want to give him to put your lights out?

Long-range shooting isn't any better for zombies. In theory, our bodily stillness could make us incredible snipers, but there is more to the equation than first meets the eye. Let's say you spot a group of freshies 300 yards away and dump one of them with a well-aimed shot. What happens then? The freshies will drag their colleague to cover and ready their own weapons. If the guy you shot dies, then his brains will be poor eating by the time you finally finish the fight. You also may be looking at a long-range shootout, which doesn't favor a force of one. The whole proposition just isn't a fit for us. Snipers are meant to stay hidden and attack from a distance; the work of a zombie is necessarily up-close and personal.

9MM - TOO SMALL TO HANDLE

Another issue with zombies using firearms is the lack of sensitivity in our hands. Having zombie hands is like doing everything with fat gloves on, and as a result, you can't feel whether or not a firearm is on "safe." The only way for a zombie to be sure is to check the safety visually, and there's no time for that when the shit hits the fan. I've also found that loading rounds into a magazine is problematic. It's not only mechanically difficult, but pieces of your skin tend to go into the magazine along with the bullets, causing frequent jams. If you insist on using a gun, I would recommend a shotgun (either a double-barrel or pump). They have nice big shells for your clumsy hands to get a hold of, and nice big holes to load them into.

12GA - EASIER TO GRIP

MAN TRAPS

HISTORICALLY, TRAPS HAVE ALWAYS BEEN AN IMPORTANT TOOL FOR THE TAKING OF WILD GAME. FOOTHOLD TRAPS, SNARE TRAPS, AND SPIKE PITS ARE AMONG THE MOST COMMONLY KNOWN, BUT THEY ARE OF LIMITED USE TO ZOMBIES. HUMAN BEINGS USUALLY HAVE THE INGENUITY TO FREE THEMSELVES WHEN GIVEN ENOUGH TIME, SO YOU CAN'T JUST PLANT A DEVICE AND LEAVE IT UNATTENDED THE WAY THAT A FUR TRAPPER WOULD. WHEN USED FOR HARRASSMENT OR AS PART OF A LARGER AMBUSH STRATEGY, THOUGH, TRAPS CAN HELP YOU GET THE JOB DONE BY ACTING AS AN "EXTRA SET OF HANDS."

USING OTHER WEAPONS

Sometimes using a cutting or cudgeling weapon can bring a quicker end to a fight, but again, it's always best if your hands are empty for grabbing your opponent. A reasonable rule would be to use these handheld weapons if you really want to, but to drop them as soon as your control of a situation becomes tenuous. When things get dodgy, you want to fall back on the safety net of your natural tools and instincts.

FINAL THOUGHTS ON HUNTING AND COMBAT

I feel like I've only scratched the surface of the subject, but the key ideas I have covered should give you a strong foundation on which to build. Keep in mind that being a good hunter means being cautious, but not timid. Go out there and be a playmaker. Get the brains you deserve.

JOURNAL ENTRIES

"HEADHUNTER LAUREATE"

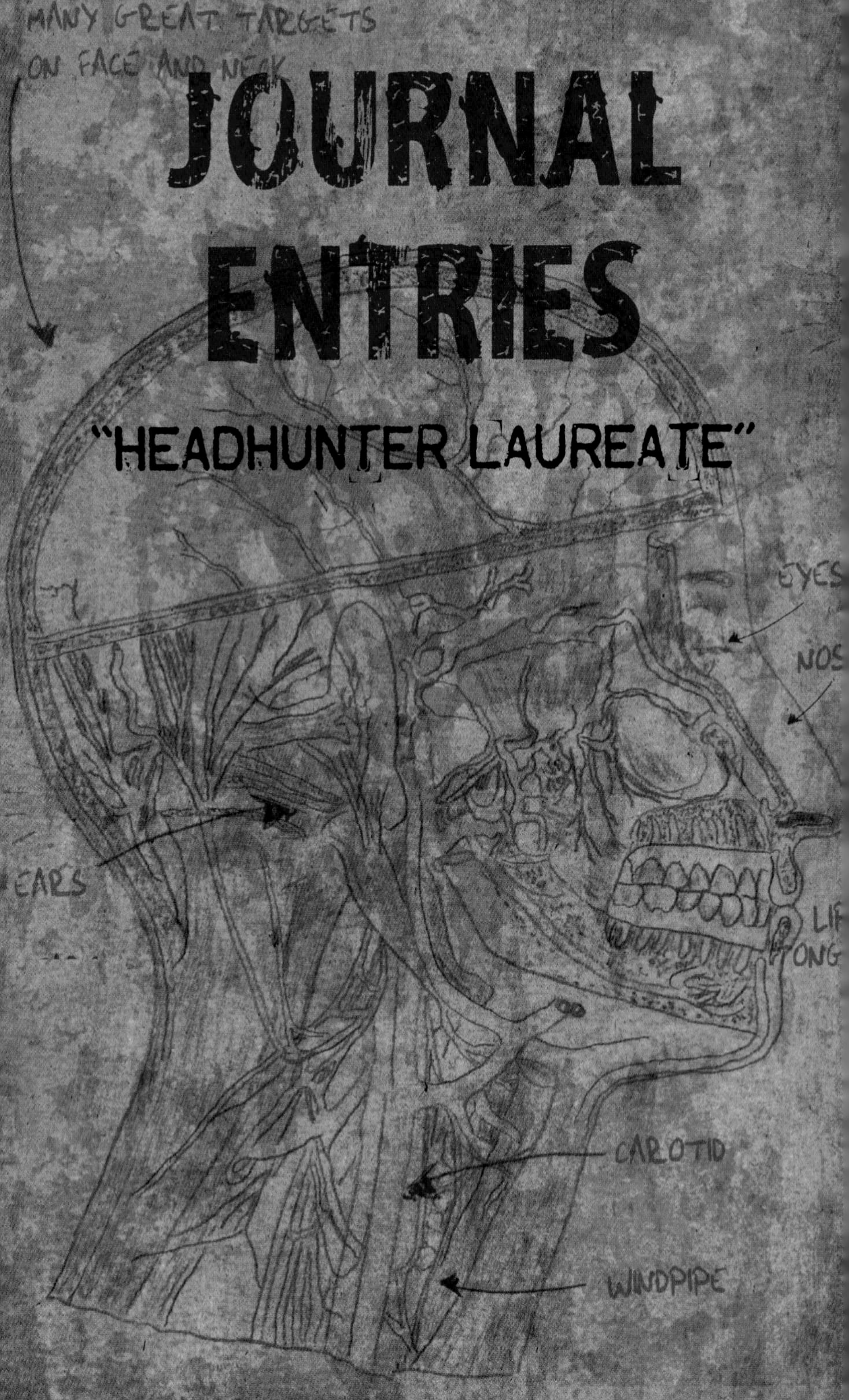

MANY GREAT TARGETS
ON FACE AND NECK

EYES

NOS

EARS

LIF
ONG

CAROTID

WINDPIPE

DAY FOUR 9:08 PM

I'M IN THE MIDDLE OF A MULTIPLE VICTIM RUN, PREYING ON HAPLESS CITIZENS WHO HAVE LOCKED THEMSELVES IN THEIR HOMES. IN EVERY CATACLYSMIC EVENT, THERE ARE ALWAYS A BUNCH OF DUMMIES WHO STAY PUT, THINKING THE GOVERNMENT WILL TAKE CARE OF EVERYTHING - IRONIC CONSIDERING IT'S USUALLY THE GOVERNMENT WHO'S RESPONSIBLE FOR THE WHOLE MESS.

DAY SEVEN 4:15 PM

I'VE COVERED A LOT OF GROUND OVER THE PAST WEEK AND HAVEN'T SEEN A SQUARE FOOT OF THIS TOWN LEFT UNTOUCHED BY THE OUTBREAK. IT RIPPED THROUGH HERE LIKE A BULL ON FIRE - PROBABLY DUE TO IGNORANCE ABOUT THE PACE INFECTION. MEDICAL AND LAW ENFORCEMENT PERSONNEL PROBABLY DEALT WITH THE REANIMATED LIKE THEY WERE PEOPLE IN NEED OF TREATMENT, AS OPPOSED TO MONSTERS THAT SHOULD BE SHOT IN THE HEAD. ZOMBIES WHO WERE BEING RESTRAINED AND TREATED WOULD HAVE HAD PLENTY OF OPPORTUNITIES TO BITE, THEREBY INFECTING THE VERY PEOPLE WHO WERE BEST EQUIPPED TO RESTORE ORDER. JUST A THEORY, OF COURSE. I'LL NEVER KNOW FOR SURE HOW IT ALL WENT DOWN. WITHOUT THE INTERNET OR CNN, I'M LEFT TO PIECE THINGS TOGETHER ONE SLIVER OF INFORMATION AT A TIME.

DAY 36 1:40 AM

IN RETROSPECT, THE WHOLE BRAIN FASTING EXPERIMENT WAS A TERRIBLE IDEA. ON THE BRIGHT SIDE, THOUGH, IT DID SHOW ME HOW MUCH I WANT TO LIVE AND HOW PRECIOUS A THING MY MIND IS. I DESERVE BETTER THAN TO DIE HUNGRY AND INSANE, HANDCUFFED TO THE BACK OF A TRACTOR. ALSO, IN MY FEVERED STATE I GAVE MYSELF A LAST NAME. I FOUND THE REMAINS OF A SHAMROCK TATTOO ON MY RIGHT CALF, WHICH TELLS ME I MAY HAVE IRISH HERITAGE, SO I

ADOPTED THE SURNAME "MCGHOUL." IT HAS A RING
TO IT AND REFLECTS BOTH MY GAELIC ROOTS AND MY
PROCLIVITY FOR EATING THE DEAD.

DAY 49 11:15 AM

THE PACK AND I TOOK OUT A WHOLE SCHOOL BUS FULL
OF PEOPLE THIS MORNING. I CAN'T TAKE MUCH CREDIT
FOR IT, THOUGH, SINCE I STUMBLED ONTO THE SCENE
WHEN MOST OF THE WORK WAS ALREADY DONE. AT
ABOUT SEVEN O'CLOCK I WAS WALKING THE STREETS,
CHECKING THE AIR FOR A WHIFF OF BRAINS, WHEN
I HEARD THE ROAR OF A ZOMBIE MOB. I ROUNDED
THE CORNER TO SEE A BROKEN DOWN SCHOOL BUS
SURROUNDED BY A SEA OF UNDEAD. A TRACE OF STEAM
WAS SEEPING OUT FROM UNDER THE VEHICLE'S HOOD,
AND ITS RIGHT FRONT RIM WAS STRIPPED BARE FROM
HAVING BEEN DRIVEN SOME DISTANCE ON A FLAT TIRE.
A GROUP OF ABOUT TEN PEOPLE HUDDLED TOGETHER
ON TOP OF THE BUS, WHILE ANOTHER DOZEN OR SO
WERE DEAD INSIDE IT. IT APPEARED THE LATTER
GROUP HAD ATTEMPTED TO LOCK THEMSELVES IN, ONLY
TO HAVE THE DOOR FORCED OPEN BY THE AGGRESSIVE
ZOMBIE HORDE.

I ALWAYS WONDER WHAT THE BACK-STORY IS WHEN
I STUMBLE ONTO A STRANGE SIGHT LIKE THAT. A
LITTLE OVER HALF THE PEOPLE ON THE ROOF WERE
YOUNG GUYS IN HIGH SCHOOL LETTER JACKETS
(BASEBALL PLAYERS), AND A FEW AMONG THE GROUP
HAD GUNS, BUT THEY WERE LONG SINCE OUT OF
AMMUNITION. IF I HAD TO GUESS, I'D SAY THE KIDS WERE
OFF AT AN AWAY GAME WHEN THE OUTBREAK HIT.
THEY PROBABLY HOLED UP FOR A WHILE SOMEPLACE
(WHERE THEY WERE JOINED BY THE RANDOM CIVIES),
THEN TRIED TO MAKE A RUN FOR ANOTHER AREA
WHEN THEIR BUS QUIT ON THEM.

HOWEVER IT CAME THE BE, THE SITUATION WAS A
STAND-OFF FOR THE MOMENT, WITH THE FRESHIES ON
THE ROOF OUT OF REACH AND THE ZOMBIES ON THE

GROUND UNABLE TO WORK THE SIMPLE PUZZLE OF HOW
TO GET AT THEM. I HUSTLED MY WAY TO THE FRONT
OF THE CROWD, HOPPED UP ONTO THE NOSE OF THE
BUS, AND THEN ONTO THE ROOF. WHAT FOLLOWED WAS
A HIGH-STAKES GAME OF "KING OF THE HILL" BETWEEN
ME AND THE YOUNG ATHLETES. I TOSSED THEM ONE
AT A TIME INTO THE PIT OF FRENZIED MAN-EATERS,
LOSING ONLY ONE CONTEST TO A TOUGH, STOCKY GUY -
PROBABLY THE TEAM'S CATCHER. FORTUNATELY, UNLIKE
MY OPPONENTS, I COULD ALWAYS CLIMB UP AND TRY
AGAIN IF I LOST. I SAVED THE LAST VICTIM FOR MYSELF
AND FELT KIND OF SORRY FOR THE KID SINCE HE DIDN'T
HAVE ANY GOOD OPTIONS. HE COULD EITHER WAIT FOR
ME TO KILL HIM OR LEAP INTO THE YAWNING MASS OF
TWISTED FACES. IN THE END, HE CHOSE THE FRYING
PAN OVER THE FIRE. HIS BRAIN HAD A FLAVOR LIKE
SLIGHTLY SPOILED ORANGE JUICE. STRANGE.

DAY 58 12:20 AM
I STOPPED IN AT AN ABANDONED GYM FOR A STRENGTH
CHECK AND WAS HAPPY TO SEE MY BENCH PRESS IS UP
TO 495 LBS. THAT'S FIVE OF THE BIG PLATES ON EACH
SIDE - PRETTY BEASTIE. I DIDN'T WANT TO PUSH IT
ANY FURTHER FOR FEAR THAT THE EQUIPMENT MIGHT
FAIL. AFTER DODGING BULLETS AND FARM IMPLEMENTS
FOR THE LAST TWO MONTHS, I WOULDN'T DIG THE
IRONY OF GETTING MY SKULL CRUSHED IN A HEALTH
CLUB ACCIDENT. LIKE IN EVERY GYM, THE PLACE HAD
MIRRORS ON THE WALLS, BUT I TRIED TO AVERT MY
EYES FROM THEM. IT'S NOT THAT I HAVE A PROBLEM
WITH WHAT I AM; I'M JUST NOT SURE I EVER WANT

TO KNOW WHAT I LOOK LIKE AGAIN. LIFE WITHOUT COMBS, TOOTHBRUSHES, AND PIMPLE CREAM HAS BEEN SO LIBERATING, I NEVER WANT TO GO BACK TO CARING ABOUT MY APPEARANCE.

DAY 60 4:15 PM
AFTER RACKING UP FOUR KILLS YESTERDAY (MY FIRST USE OF LIVE, HUMAN BAIT), I'M ON THE PROWL AGAIN TODAY. MAN, THERE ARE DEAD BODIES EVERYWHERE. YOU STOP NOTICING THEM AFTER A WHILE. IT'S KIND OF LIKE THE DARK SPOTS ON A CITY SIDEWALK FROM DECADES OF PEOPLE DROPPING THEIR CHEWING GUM. YOUR EYES DON'T SEE THEM ANYMORE UNTIL YOU REALLY LOOK, AND WHEN YOU FINALLY DO, YOU REALIZE THERE ARE TOO MANY TO COUNT. MOST OF THE DEAD ARE VICTIMS WHO HAD THEIR BRAINS EATEN, LEAVING THEM INCAPABLE OF REANIMATION, AND SOME DIED SO LONG AGO THEY HAVE THAT FLAT, ROAD KILL LOOK WITH THEIR CLOTHING PASTED TO THE GROUND BY WEATHER. IT SEEMS LIKE JUST YESTERDAY THE WHOLE THING STARTED... SPEAKING OF WHICH, I'VE OFFICIALLY FORGOTTEN WHERE I PUT MY FILE BOX FROM THE LABORATORY. I KEPT TRACK, FOR A WHILE, OF THE VARIOUS PLACES I STOWED IT, BUT EVENTUALLY I WANDERED TOO FAR AWAY FROM IT AND LET TOO MUCH TIME ELAPSE. BRAIN FIXATION WILL DO THAT TO YOU. I STILL HAVE THE CAMERA, THOUGH, AND HAVE BEEN TAKING A LOT OF GOOD PICTURES.

DAY 63 11:20 PM
WHEN THE SKY IS CLEAR, LIKE IT IS TONIGHT, I'LL LIE ON MY BACK FOR HOURS LOOKING UP AT THE STARS. KEEPING MY BODY COMPLETELY STILL, AND WITHOUT THE DISTRACTIONS OF BREATH OR A HEARTBEAT, I FEEL LIKE A BEING OF PURE CONSCIOUSNESS. I WONDER IF GOD HAS A BRAIN.

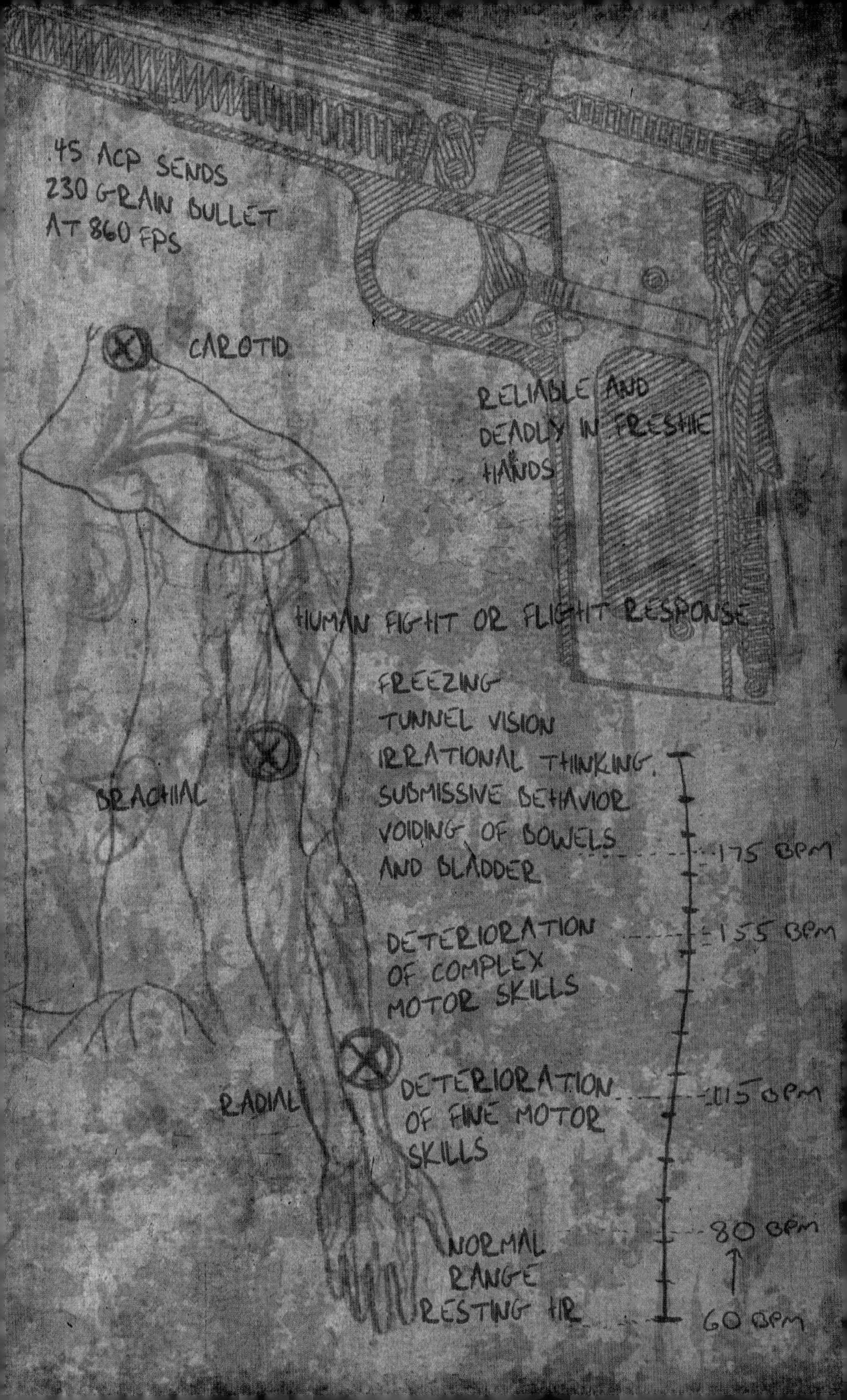

.45 ACP SENDS
230 GRAIN BULLET
AT 860 FPS

CAROTID

RELIABLE AND
DEADLY IN FRESHIE
HANDS

HUMAN FIGHT OR FLIGHT RESPONSE

FREEZING
TUNNEL VISION
IRRATIONAL THINKING
SUBMISSIVE BEHAVIOR
VOIDING OF BOWELS ----- 175 BPM
AND BLADDER

BRACHIAL

DETERIORATION ----- 155 BPM
OF COMPLEX
MOTOR SKILLS

RADIAL

DETERIORATION ----- 115 BPM
OF FINE MOTOR
SKILLS

NORMAL ----- 80 BPM
RANGE ↑
RESTING HR ----- 60 BPM

CHAPTER 4

KNOW YOUR ENEMY

"Man, I can assure you, is a nasty animal."

- Molière

YOUR OPPOSITION IN WAR

I don't have any love for
the freshies as a whole.
They really are a bunch of
bastards. "Human beings"
and "homo sapiens" are more
formal names for them, but
I usually refer to them by
nicknames like "freshies,"
"bleeders," "breathers,"
"runners," "pinkskins," "brain
steaks," or "self-propelled
breakfast." Remember that
they are more than simply
creatures that you dislike;
they are an enemy force
whose strengths, weaknesses,
and capabilities you must
intimately understand.

SIZING THEM UP

When you've acquired enough field experience, you'll be
able to assess the threat a freshie poses by observing his
physical appearance and body movements. You'll acquire a
feel for your enemy the same way a zoologist gets a feel

for animals after spending a lot of time in the wild. Here are some indicators that I have found useful in judging the danger your enemy presents:

Posture
Rolled-in shoulders and a forward-pitching head are signs of weakness - manifestations of low self-esteem and years of unconscious cowering. These characteristics betray a personality that will fold in a stressful situation. Distention of the stomach implies poor muscular strength in the abdomen and lower back, and correlates negatively with athletic ability. Though a freshie who stands confidently is not necessarily a competent fighter, his posture is a warning to prepare for the worst.

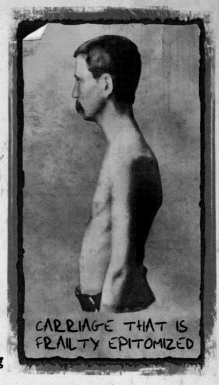

CARRIAGE THAT IS FRAILTY EPITOMIZED

A MORE CHALLENGING FRAME TO TACKLE

Musculature
Muscle definition doesn't tell you anything about combat skill but is obviously a sign of strength. It's worth mentioning that men with the highest levels of combat training are usually not that heavily muscled. Members of a SWAT team may be huge and buff, but guys like the Navy SEALs are usually medium-sized and non-descript-looking.

Nervous Mannerisms
Among combat beginners you will see darting eyes, nail biting, incessant weapon checking, and a lot of turning to comrades for information and reassurance. I was

stalking a guy once who looked like a badass '80s action hero, but when he kept on stroking his mustache, I knew he had a heart of jell-o. Nervousness is greatest among the most poorly prepared.

Professional Bearing

Expert soldiers move with confident poise. They have a smooth, precise way about them that only comes from extensive training. You will know it as soon as you see it - just like you can tell a good dancer from a bad one even if you don't know anything about dancing. If you see even one man in a group possessing this predatory grace, give them a wide berth.

Compensating Behavior

Screaming and other broad shows of bravado from your opponent mean that he is an easy mark. They are clear indications that he does not know his way around a fight and is trying to assuage his own fear. Freshies will also sometimes "play soldier" to make themselves feel better about their tactical ignorance. If you see a group acting like hotshots - moving in awkward formations or communicating with cheap hand signals - that's even better for you than a group that's openly clueless. Pretenders have just enough false confidence to walk themselves into a tough situation, only to fall apart when the fur starts flying.

HUMAN WEAPONRY

Mankind is a belligerent breed, and the weapons they have at their disposal are many and varied. In the interest of brevity, I will cover only those weapons that are most frequently encountered - the types used by civilians and police. (If you are facing military forces, you are in for a fight of another order and will need special instruction not contained in this book.)

HAND JIVE

THIS IS THE MILITARY HAND SIGNAL FOR "FREEZE" THAT SHOWS UP IN ALL OF THE MOVIES. COMBAT POSEURS USE THIS ONE ALL OF THE TIME, SO IF A FRESHIE FLASHES IT, WATCH HIM MORE CLOSELY FOR SIGNS OF INEXPERIENCE.

HANDGUNS

There are an estimated 70 million privately owned handguns in the United States, which means you are going to see them just about everywhere. Here are the major types:

<u>Back-up Handguns</u> (calibers .22 Short to .380 ACP)
Designed for portability and ease of concealment, these weapons represent about half of all civilian handguns. They are a limited threat, being both inaccurate (usually equipped with crude sights) and low in stopping power. Their rounds are so weak, in fact, they may even ricochet off of your skull if they strike your head at an oblique angle. The biggest danger these weapons present is that they can appear out of nowhere from the pocket of a seemingly unarmed opponent.

BACK-UP HANDGUNS: 1. COLT COBRA (.22 LR, 2-SHOT)
2. ASTRA CUB (.22 SHORT, 6-SHOT) 3. RUGER LCP (.380 ACP, 6-SHOT) 4. PHOENIX ARMS P-25 (.25 ACP, 6-SHOT)
4. S&W AIRLITE PD (.22 WMR, 7-SHOT)

Medium Caliber Handguns (calibers 9mm to .45 ACP)
These law enforcement and military-grade handguns
are America's weapons of choice for personal defense.
Penetration of your skull is no problem for their heavier
ammunition, and the wound channel they create - especially
with hollow point bullets - poses a substantial risk to your
safety. In addition, guns like these often have a magazine
capacity in the double digits, giving a freshie plenty of
chances to hit the jackpot and put you down for good.
While a .45 or a 9mm hollow point strike to your torso will
do you no harm, it will impel you backwards with the force
of a good, solid punch. Fully jacketed rounds, on the other
hand, will just zip through your body unnoticed (unless
they strike a bone).

MEDIUM CALIBER PISTOLS: 1. SPRINGFIELD M1911A1 (.45
ACP, 7-SHOT W/STANDARD MAG.) 2. BERETTA 92F (9MM,
15-SHOT) 3. WALTHER P99-C (.40 S&W, 8-SHOT)

MEDIUM CALIBER REVOLVERS: 1. RUGER GP100 (.357 MAG, 6-SHOT) 2. S&W MODEL 40 (.38 SPECIAL, 5-SHOT)

<u>Large Caliber Handguns</u> (calibers .44 Mag. to .50 AE)
Seen in the Dirty Harry and Death Wish movies, these handguns were intended to be collector novelties or self-defense weapons against bears and other large wilderness predators. While such big handguns are not very practical in combat (the recoil is brutal), they do quite a number when they score a hit. A gun like this could blow your head to pieces, and what's worse, even hits to your limbs can be disabling. If someone shoots you in the knee with a .454 Casull, you could lose your lower leg and be forced to finish the fight scrambling around on the ground. Fortunately, large-caliber "hand cannons" are rare compared to their lower-powered counterparts.

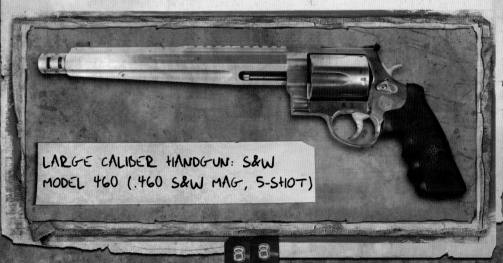

LARGE CALIBER HANDGUN: S&W MODEL 460 (.460 S&W MAG, 5-SHOT)

SUBMACHINE GUNS

These weapons are rarely encountered outside of military duty since their fully automatic capability makes them illegal for most people to own. They can be found in the hands of **SWAT** teams, though, and sometimes in the lockers of specially licensed civilians. Chambered for medium caliber pistol ammunition, submachine guns can fire at a rate of 600-800 rounds per minute, presenting an extra level of danger to your cranium. One squeeze of the trigger will send three or four bullets in your direction with surprising accuracy. These weapons are also short in length, making them easier for your opponents to handle in tight spaces and harder for you to grab away from them in a tussle.

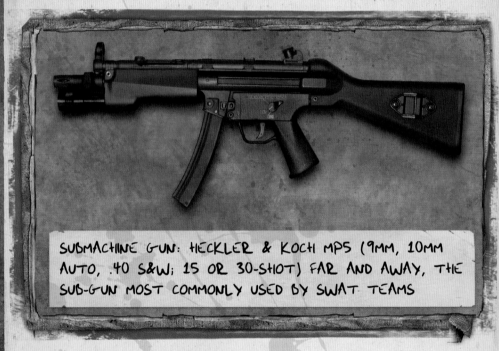

SUBMACHINE GUN: HECKLER & KOCH MP5 (9MM, 10MM AUTO, .40 S&W; 15 OR 30-SHOT) FAR AND AWAY, THE SUB-GUN MOST COMMONLY USED BY SWAT TEAMS

RIFLES AND CARBINES

Referred to as "long guns" for their size, these weapons have a greater sight radius (the distance between the front and rear sights) than pistols, and are therefore more accurate and dangerous at ranges over 30ft. They are clumsy at close quarters, though, so crowd a guy with a rifle in an indoor fight and you've got the upper hand.

Light Sporting Rifles (usually .22 caliber)

I use this category as a catch-all for rifles used in recreational plinking. The most common among them seem to be .22 caliber repeaters, but a handful are carbines chambered for different types of pistol ammunition. Magazine capacity can be anywhere from four to thirty rounds. A lot of times these weapons look like glorified BB guns, but don't be fooled - they are capable of rapid, accurate fire. A twelve year-old boy scout once pinned me down behind a tool shed for an hour with a .22 rifle. Every time I tried running, he sent bullets in the direction of my head, many of which ripped into my neck and shoulders. That big-eared S.O.B. could shoot.

LIGHT SPORTING RIFLES: 1. CZ MODEL 452 (.22 LR, 5-SHOT) 2. RUGER 77/22 ALL-WEATHER (.22 LR, 10-SHOT) 3. RUGER 10/22 (.22 LR, 10-SHOT) 4. HENRY REPEATING ARMS H001 (.22 LR, 15-SHOT)

Assault-Type Rifles (usually .223, .308, or 7.62x39 caliber)
These rifles represent the standard issue weapons of
military forces worldwide for the last fifty years, and
semi-automatic versions of them are found in some
civilian homes (an estimated 1.5 million are privately
owned). You're often facing a magazine capacity of 30
rounds in these weapons, and the potential for accurate
fire on a head-sized target at over 100yds. Their bullets
will penetrate the skull bone effortlessly, even punching
through helmets and flak vests. SWAT teams may be
equipped with assault rifles capable of fully-automatic fire.

ASSAULT-TYPE RIFLES: 1. S&W M&P15 (.223 REM, 20
OR 30-SHOT) 2. AK-47 (7.62X39, 20 OR 30-SHOT)
3. SPRINGFIELD SOCOM II (.308 WIN, 10 OR 20-SHOT)
4. RUGER MINI-14 (.223 REM, 10, 20, OR 30-SHOT)

Hunting and Sniper Rifles (calibers .223 to .458 Win. Mag.)
These scoped rifles are usually bolt-action and come in a
variety of chamberings to bring down anything from a
gopher to a 2000-pound African Buffalo. Their hallmark
is accuracy at long ranges - up to 1000 yards for some -
which means big trouble for us. A decent shooter with
one of these rifles can make easy head shots from several
hundred yards away, taking out as many slow movers
as he has bullets without a zombie ever getting close.
Seeing a scoped hunting rifle always makes me mad; it's
as if they're not just dangerous, but culturally offensive.
Consider it your solemn obligation as a zombie to stalk and
kill any freshie you see running around with one of these
tack drivers.

HUNTING AND SNIPER RIFLES: 1. ACCURACY INTER-
NATIONAL AE (.308 WIN, 5 OR 10-SHOT) 2. SAVAGE
MODEL 10 (.308 WIN, 4-SHOT) 3. MOSSBERG 100 ATR
(30-06, 4-SHOT)

SHOTGUNS

There is one shotgun for every four adults in the United States, and at short range these weapons are the gods of war. A standard 12-gauge buckshot round holds nine lead pellets, each about .33 caliber in size, and at distances from 10-30yds the pellets spread out in a circular pattern, increasing the likelihood that a freshie will score a hit to your head. At point-blank range the pellets stay in a tight group, meaning a hit will blast a "rat hole" through your body with all nine pellets. If I lift up my shirt, you can see daylight coming through the area of my right kidney - the result of one of my many run-ins with shotguns.

Double-Barreled Shotguns

These are perhaps the most common civilian firearms in the world and are especially abundant in rural areas. Any time you enter a farmhouse, assume that the occupants have one. These weapons have two triggers - one for each barrel - giving the shooter the option of firing one barrel at a time or both at once. In my opinion, this is an advantage for us. In the excitement of a life-or-death situation, many people will fire both barrels right away due to the adrenaline coursing through their system. To reload, they then have to "break open" the weapon and insert fresh cartridges into the breach. This process is time consuming and difficult to execute under extreme pressure, giving you the window you need to close the gap and put them to bed.

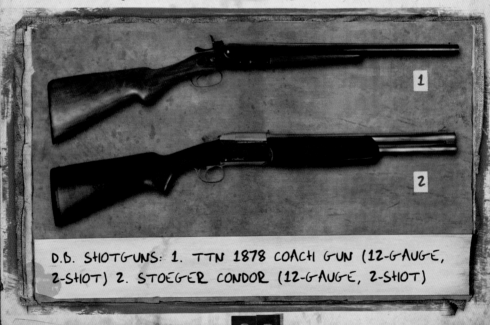

D.B. SHOTGUNS: 1. TTN 1878 COACH GUN (12-GAUGE, 2-SHOT) 2. STOEGER CONDOR (12-GAUGE, 2-SHOT)

Pump Shotguns

Pump shotguns are popular for both sporting and law enforcement purposes, and are characterized by the "pump" mechanism that ejects a spent cartridge and chambers a new one. They typically hold 4-8 rounds in a tubular magazine below the barrel. While a trained user with this weapon will give you fits, an inexperienced one can be an easy kill. In the heat of battle, novice operators often make a mistake called "short-stroking," which is a failure to pull the pump mechanism all the way to the rear before pushing it forward again. This causes a weapon malfunction that is a hassle to clear. If you see someone with a pump shotgun fire a round, pump the weapon, and then struggle with it, you know you have a good several seconds to close the distance without taking fire.

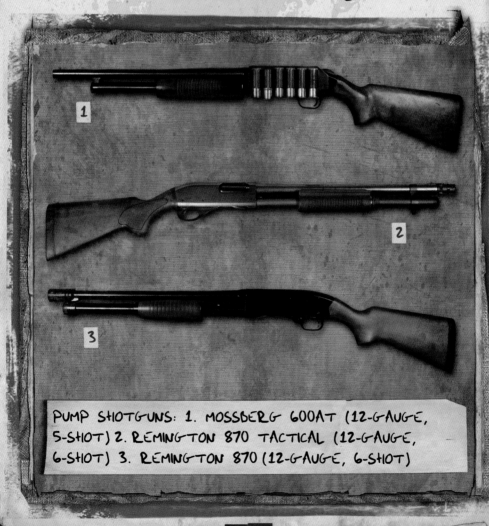

PUMP SHOTGUNS: 1. MOSSBERG 600AT (12-GAUGE, 5-SHOT) 2. REMINGTON 870 TACTICAL (12-GAUGE, 6-SHOT) 3. REMINGTON 870 (12-GAUGE, 6-SHOT)

Auto-Loading Shotguns

Similar in size and magazine capacity to pump shotguns, the autoloaders have the advantage of firing semi-automatically, discharging rounds as fast as you can pull the trigger. Also like the pumps, these weapons have both sporting and law enforcement applications. Fortunately, the recoil of a shotgun blast is pretty severe, and accurate, rapid fire with an auto-loader is far more difficult than with the average rifle or carbine. I consider this weapon the deadliest to zombiekind in close encounters.

AUTO-LOADING SHOTGUNS: 1. REMINGTON 11 A (12-GAUGE, 4-SHOT) 2. BENELLI M4 (12-GAUGE, 7-SHOT)

BOWS AND ARROWS

Only about one in one hundred Americans knows how to hunt with a bow, so I won't get into much detail on the various types. As a rule, you'll want to treat bows with the same respect as you would a slow, single-shot firearm. Crossbows and compound bows will easily drive an arrow - even one with a broadhead hunting tip - right through your skull. Less powerful re-curve bows can be dangerous as well, but only when using arrows with narrower heads (like bullet and field tips). Small pistol crossbows are handy for freshies to carry but would have to put a bolt right through your eye socket to have any effect. A word of advice concerning bows: if you're minding your own business and suddenly hear a snapping sound - similar to

someone slapping a quarter on a tile floor, or breaking
a plastic rod in half - there's a chance that someone has
just fired an arrow at you. Move your head immediately
because you've only got a fraction of a second before the
projectile arrives.

THROWN WEAPONS

When closing in on human prey, you'll get all kinds of
objects tossed at you. I've found that most of these things
- even the seemingly dangerous ones - are pretty harmless.

Knives, Axes and Spears

Throwing these weapons is a very specific skill that
requires a great deal of practice to master. Only a handful
of people - like circus performers and survivalists - do
it well enough to be dangerous. In addition, the weapons
these experts use are often balanced especially for
throwing. The average freshie hurling kitchen cutlery and
homemade spears at you will be both too unskilled and too
poorly equipped to succeed. Among the axes and knives
I've had thrown at me, none of them ever hit my head, and
the ones that hit my body never hit blade-first.

Molotov Cocktails

The biggest problem freshies have with Molotov cocktails is
that glass bottles are sturdy and don't tend to break when
they hit you directly. They will often break when they
impact the ground nearby, but the splash will only set your
legs on fire - not a big deal. The only Molotov cocktail
that ever gave me a scare was one made from a gallon
wine jug that was tossed down at me from the roof of a
convenience store. That case was an unusual combination
of a large volume of fuel and a high-velocity impact.

Pipe Bombs

Unlike with a government-issue grenade, a pipe bomb
explosion creates very inconsistent fragmentation. The
nuts, bolts and nails strapped to it will go flying at deadly
speed, but the chances of one of them sailing through your
E-node are pretty slim. If someone throws a pipe bomb at
you, just move away from it as quickly as you can. The
fuse will probably allow you plenty of time to clear the
blast radius. If it looks like it might go off right away,
jump on it and smother the explosion with your belly.
What it does to your vestigial guts won't be pretty, but
your head will be protected, and it won't hurt a bit.

SWUNG WEAPONS

In close combat, implements that are swung like a hammer, as opposed to those thrust like a spear, are the least effective against zombies. Since these weapons travel along an arc, the distance they must cover is greater, making them slower in action and easier to block with your arms. In addition, they usually attack in a downward motion, striking your cranium on the top where it is the most robust. The heavier and more destructive the swung weapon, the more unwieldy it tends to be to use. A six-pound sledgehammer, for instance, would completely wreck your skull if it hit you, but you'll never be standing in one place long enough for that to happen. I rank the climbing axe as the swung weapon most hazardous to zombies. It is light, quick, and equipped with a nasty back spike that will punch into your head like a can opener.

1. ROCK HAMMER (13 IN, 1.9 LBS) - BUILT TOUGH FOR POUNDING ON ROCKS AND HAS A LONG, SHARP END THAT'S IDEAL FOR PENETRATING SKULLS.

2. CLAW HAMMER (16 IN, 1.8 LBS) - A COMMON CHOICE FOR FRESHIES; THIS PARTICULAR ONE IS SLOWER THAN AVERAGE DUE TO THE LENGTH OF ITS HANDLE.

3. STRAIGHT RAZOR (9.5 IN, 1.25 OZ) - AN ENEMY ATTACKING YOU WITH ONE OF THESE MAY AS WELL BE USING A FEATHER DUSTER.

4. SICKLE (18.5 IN, 12 OZ) - WICKED IN APPEARANCE, BUT DOESN'T HAVE ENOUGH BLADE WEIGHT TO CUT THROUGH YOUR NECK BONE.

5. CAMPING HATCHET (13 IN, 1.5 LBS) - REQUIRES A PRETTY STOUT SWING FOR IT TO GET FAR ENOUGH THROUGH YOUR SKULL TO DAMAGE YOUR E-NODE.

6. UNKNOWN HAND TOOL (15 IN, 1.25 LBS) - I HAVE NO IDEA WHAT THIS THING IS, BUT IT LOOKS LIKE IT WAS DESIGNED TO LOBOTOMIZE ZOMBIES.

7. MEAT CLEAVER (12 IN, 15 OZ) - YOU MAY LOSE FINGERS TO THIS WEAPON, BUT NOT MUCH ELSE.

1. MACHETE (29 IN, 1.2 LBS) - A DOWNRIGHT NASTY CUTTING WEAPON THAT'S THE CLOSEST THING TO A SWORD YOU'RE LIKELY TO ENCOUNTER. IT'S DESIGNED TO HACK THROUGH BRANCHES (WHICH ARE A LOT LIKE BONES), SO NEVER LET A MACHETE COME FLASHING IN AT YOUR NECK.

2. FIRE AXE (36 IN, 7.5 LBS) - SWINGS ON A VERY WIDE ARC WITH ALL OF THE WEIGHT AT THE END, MAKING IT SLOW AS MOLASSES IN BATTLE. IF SOMEONE SWINGS ONE AT YOU, DON'T STEP BACK, STEP IN TO PUT THE DESCENDING AXE HEAD BEHIND YOU.

3. HIGH-TEST CHAIN (48 IN, 3.5 LBS) - NOT A LETHAL DANGER, BUT CAN BE SWUNG TO WRAP AROUND YOUR LIMBS, THUS TRIPPING YOU OR IMMOBILIZING AN ARM; CAN ALSO BE FOLDED IN HALF AND SWUNG, DOUBLING ITS IMPACT WEIGHT.

4. BAILING HOOK (11 IN, 1.5 LBS) - IMPRESSIVE SPEED AND PENETRATING POWER. WHEN A BAILING HOOK IS COMING DOWN TOWARD YOUR HEAD, MOVE LATERALLY JUST ENOUGH TO TAKE THE BLOW ON YOUR SHOULDER; THE WEAPON WILL LIKELY STICK AND BE DIFFICULT TO WITHDRAW.

5. CARPENTER'S HATCHET (13 IN, 1.5 LBS) - SEE "CAMPING HATCHET."

6. SAWED-OFF BASEBALL BAT (23 IN, 1.6 LBS) - AN ADOLESCENT'S ALUMINUM BAT MODIFIED WITH A HACKSAW AND GORILLA TAPE TO BECOME A ONE-HANDED WEAPON. IT DOESN'T HAVE THE MASS TO DO YOU IN WITH ONE BLOW, BUT BECOMES A THREAT ONCE YOUR SKULL BONE HAS BEEN BROKEN.

7. CAST IRON SKILLET (16 IN, 4.5 LBS) - HEAVY AND POORLY BALANCED WITH A HANDLE THAT HAS TERRIBLE ERGONOMICS FOR COMBAT. THAT'S NOT TO SAY IT'S NOT DANGEROUS; A STRONG MAN WIELDING ONE OF THESE EDGE-FIRST CAN DEFINITELY DASH OUT THE CONTENTS OF YOUR CRANIUM.

THRUSTING WEAPONS

Among melee weapons, those that are thrust in a straight line possess the greatest penetrative power, making them the most likely to get through your cranial bones and pierce your E-node. The ice pick and the sharpened screwdriver are the most dangerous of this type held in one hand. A gleaming, Rambo-style hunting knife may look intimidating, but trust me when I say it's nothing compared to a five-dollar Phillips Head. The two-handed thrusting weapons, though, are the most fearsome since they allow the attacker to use not just his arm strength, but the full weight of his body; bayonets and sharpened spades are good examples of these. I once faced a freshie who had taken a pitchfork and cut off all of the prongs except for those in the middle, which concentrated all of the force of the blow on the two remaining points. He iced four slow movers in about six seconds before I finally put a stop to it. As a rule, you need to be most concerned about weapons that focus the greatest amount of force on the smallest surface area and are quickest in action.

1. SHARPENED GARDEN SPADE (38 IN, 4.4 LBS) - CUTTING THE CORNERS OFF OF ITS BLADE HAS TURNED THIS SPADE INTO THE PERFECT HEAD WRECKER.

2. BAYONET (14.5 IN, 15 OZ) - UNBELIEVABLY DANGEROUS WHEN FASTENED TO THE END OF A BATTLE RIFLE.

3. CROWBAR (30 IN, 4.1 LBS) - HAND-MADE GRIPS ALLOW FOR FIRMER THRUSTS.

4. MODIFIED SPADING FORK (40 IN, 3.5 LBS) - I WAS GLAD TO GET THIS ZOMBIE KILLER OFF THE STREETS.

5. SCREWDRIVERS (8.5-11.5 IN, 4-6 OZ) - STIFF, STURDY, AND DEADLY THRUSTING WEAPONS.

6. TIRE REAMER (5.5 IN, 2.3 OZ) - A T-SHAPED GRIP MEANS THE FRESHIES CAN YOU PUNCH WITH IT.

7. SCISSORS (13 IN, 11 OZ) - MORE EFFECTIVE WHEN THE SCREW IS REMOVED AND ONLY A SINGLE BLADE IS USED.

8. KITCHEN KNIFE (13 IN, 3.5 OZ) - THIS MODEL IS TOO LIGHT AND FLIMSY TO PRESENT ANY THREAT.

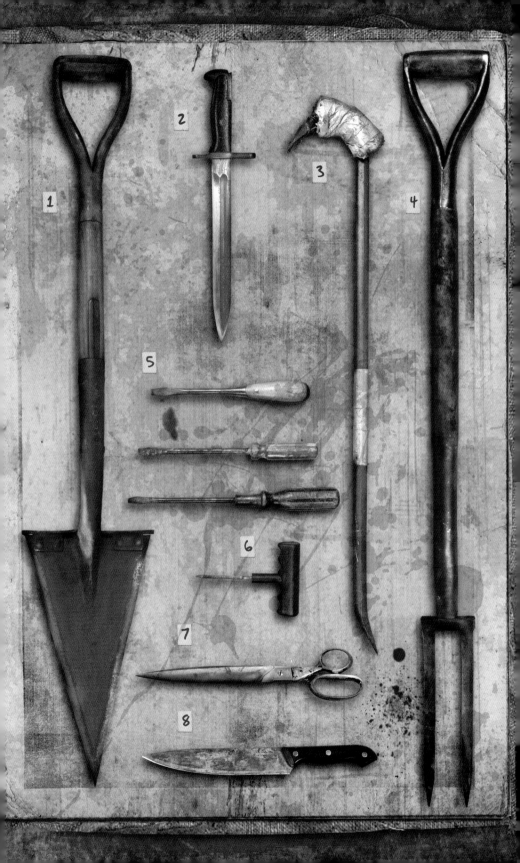

HUMAN COMBAT TRAINING

The type of weapon a freshie is holding matters far less than how well he is able to use it. Here are some statistics I dug up to give you an idea how many adult Americans have been taught to kill:

1 in 117 is a current member of the military stationed in U.S. This estimate includes National Guard and reserve troops. While Navy, Air Force, and Coast Guard personnel are not heavily drilled in ground combat, they are at least taught how to properly use a rifle and how to remain composed in stressful situations. Lucky for us, all of them put together are still not enough. If there are 1.7 million active duty service people in the United States (another half-a-million are currently overseas), and if every man in the field requires seven more behind the scenes to provide logistical support, that only leaves about 212,000 properly supplied troops to execute the fight. It took 14,000 National Guardsmen and Marines to restore order in a single area of Los Angeles during the riots of 1992, so doing some rough math tells me there are enough troops in the U.S. to manage chaos in just fifteen cities. And what's going on now isn't your garden-variety riot. In this case, human lawlessness is accompanied by a plague, cannibalism, and unprecedented panic, meaning the military is hopelessly overmatched. Making matters even worse for them is that many active duty service people have gone AWOL to address the needs of their own families in the crisis.

1 in 8 is a veteran of military service. A lot of veterans have become enfeebled by age, but those who have seen combat overseas are sometimes more formidable opponents than their younger, active duty counterparts.

1 in 222 is a law enforcement officer. Like members of the military, many in the law enforcement community have left their posts to tend to their families, so they won't often be operating together in units. They are all trained to handle themselves in a firefight, but their combat experience varies widely depending on the cities and neighborhoods in which they worked.

1 in 74 is a retired law enforcement officer. Being a police officer is a career, which means that these guys have had decades of experience before retiring. As a result, their decision-making ability under duress is very strong.

1 in 10 is an active sport hunter. This is a truly frightening statistic. Sport hunters have experience with concealing themselves, covering their scent, waiting patiently for their prey to appear, and shooting with emphasis on first-round accuracy. That's a hell of a combination. The  one thing we zombies have going for us is that white-tailed deer don't eat human brains, and that's a game changer. Not everyone has the mettle to set themselves up in a tree stand knowing that zombies may swarm by the hundreds and surround them, leaving no possibility of escape.

As you can see, considering some overlap of these categories, about 10% of freshies have had formal combat training, and about 15% know how to shoot. That's good news until you consider how many slow movers each of those capable gunmen could destroy in a day: plan on one zombie KIA for every three or four bullets in a skilled enemy's possession.

THE HUMAN FEAR RESPONSE

BLACKBEARD HAD THE "PRISON YARD STARE"

Why did Vlad Dracula turn his Turkish prisoners into a forest of impaled bodies? Why did Blackbeard enter battle with bits of burning rope woven into his hair? Because these men knew they could render their enemies helpless by making them feel fear. When human beings experience sheer terror, their sympathetic nervous systems activate the "body alarm" response, also known as the "fight or flight" response. Heart rate increases, and blood is directed to large muscle masses, while circulation to extremities is reduced. This response was perfect for cavemen because it helped them run faster from threats and fight more ferociously with their limbs. For modern freshie combatants, though, fight or flight isn't so hot. When their heart rate reaches 175 beats per minute - and it usually will in a close-quarters fight - their thinking becomes cloudy and their complex motor skills erode. Use of proper weapon technique becomes almost impossible. Drawing a sidearm and deactivating the safety with clumsy, shaking hands will take an inordinate amount of time, and aiming with gun sights will be out of the question. This is exactly where you want your opponent to be, and in order to best elicit this reaction, your attack should have three qualities: surprise, speed, and horror.

1) Surprise - The fear response is magnified when the threat presented is unexpected, so get as close as you can before revealing your presence, and engage in a way that is startling. Don't enter a room; explode into it. Don't pop out from behind a tree; climb the tree and drop down on your prey from above. The resulting "Oh, shit!" moment will help jack up your enemy's heart rate.

2) Speed - Always move at your maximum effective speed - the quickest you can get around without tripping over your own feet. When freshies have insufficient time to process a life-or-death situation, it exacerbates their panic. For this reason, you never want to stand and square off with your opponent; instead you want to sprint right at them and initiate body contact immediately. Attack the way those cops used to when they tackled pedophiles on "To Catch a Predator."

3) Horror - This part is all about the display. Freshies are already sickened by your appearance, and joining the ranks of the slow-moving infected is their worst nightmare. But fear-wise you can always up the ante from there. Try screaming and snarling as you close the distance, or tossing a severed head into your opponent's lap. Maybe drape some guts around your neck before you engage - anything that will widen their eyes a little.

MY WAR FACE - THE LAST THING MANY OF MY VICTIMS SEE

People with extensive training or combat experience are not as affected by the fight or flight response, so they'll take some extra tweaking. And be advised that at a heart rate of up to 110 beats per minute, human motor skills actually improve, so you can't just make your enemies afraid, you have to make them really afraid.

HUMAN VULNERABILITIES

As I have already stated, freshies have weaknesses in every part of their anatomy, but since zombies primarily attack with their teeth, I'll focus on areas of the human body that are most sensitive to bites.

Eyes

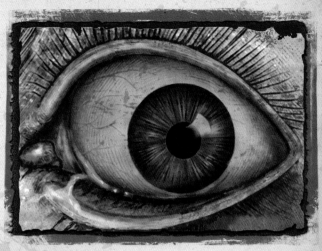

You probably won't do damage to the eyeball proper when biting at this area, but chewing off the eyebrow or eyelid will still get the job done. Blood flowing from the wound will render that eye blind, and when one eye suffers a severe trauma, the other will close reflexively. Now you've got an opponent who is in a lot of pain and can't see.

Ears, Nose, Mouth, and Genitals

These areas are all highly vascular and packed with nerve endings, meaning that bites to them will result in profuse bleeding and excruciating pain. Though attacks to these locations are rarely lethal, they have a huge psychological impact that can result in panic or even shock. This will set you up beautifully for a second, more deadly attack. Few people can think clearly after you've bitten off their nose.

Carotid Arteries

Located on either side of the throat, the carotids are the largest supplier of blood to the brain, so biting through one gets quick results. Unlike with a clean cut, the rough tear caused by a bite doesn't allow the artery's self-sealing mechanism, or tamponod, to work. Your opponent is left to choose between letting the wound bleed unabated or using one of his hands to apply pressure, both of which are poor options when fighting off a motivated zombie. Note that the carotids are under a couple of layers of muscle, so make your neck bites nice and deep. Without pressure, a torn carotid causes dizziness and weakness in 1 minute, inability to stand in 2 minutes, and full bleed-out in about 15 minutes.

Humeral Arteries

I've always felt these were underrated targets (found on the inside of each upper arm) since they are large and close to the heart; that's bad news for anyone who has a humeral artery torn. Accessibility of the humeral depends upon the girth of your victim - bigger freshies require bigger bites. Without pressure, a torn humeral causes dizziness and weakness in 3 minutes, inability to stand in 6 minutes, and full bleed out in about 45 minutes.

Carotid

Humeral

Radial

Femoral

Popliteal

Radial Artery

This is the artery that people cut when attempting suicide by slashing their wrists. Look for it on the thumb side of the inner forearm. Biting through one will not likely cause death on its own, but the blood loss and psychological effects will both be substantial. Without pressure, a torn radial causes dizziness and weakness in 6 minutes, and inability to stand in twelve minutes.

Femoral Arteries

The femoral arteries are located on the inside front of each thigh, making them a possible target if you've taken someone down by the legs. They are most accessible high in the groin and will require a whopper bite to reach any lower down. Without pressure, a torn femoral causes dizziness and weakness in 3 minutes, inability to stand in 6 minutes, and full bleed out in about 45 minutes.

Popliteal Arteries

Located behind the knees, these arteries make good targets if your enemy is on the ground facing down. As with the humerals, accessibility of the popliteals is girth-dependent, with bigger victims requiring bigger bites. A nice thing about their awkward location is that treating them with pressure is almost impossible for your victim while he is standing and on the move. Without pressure, a torn popliteal causes dizziness and weakness in 4 minutes, inability to stand in 8 minutes, and full bleed out in 60 minutes.

Jugular Vein

People always talk about the jugular vein when describing a worst-case throat injury, but the jugular carries blood at much lower pressure than the arteries, so the effect of damaging it is not as acute. It is much closer to the surface, though, and is slightly easier to tear. I look at the jugular as a bonus target, since you can get it along with the common carotid when taking a deep bite out of the right side of the throat. Without pressure, a torn jugular causes dizziness and weakness in 7 minutes, inability to stand in 14 minutes, and full bleed out in about 60 minutes.

PUSHING YOUR PREY'S HEAD UP OR TO THE SIDE EXPOSES HIS JUGULAR VEIN

It usually takes bites to two of the above-mentioned locations to guarantee taking an opponent out of the fight. A freshie may suck it up and keep battling after having his ear bitten off, but he will be done when the next bite is to a major artery. The horror of it all will overwhelm him and he'll succumb to psychogenic shock.

THEIR OWN WORST ENEMY

We would never have a chance against humanity if people didn't create so many problems for themselves. Freshies are very predictable that way - their veneer of civility vanishes and they turn on each other as soon as the rule of law loses its grip. They become selfish, violent, greedy, and destructive, and it doesn't take a catastrophe for that side of them to come out. If their local sports franchise wins a championship, they'll celebrate by fighting, destroying community property, and crippling the capital assets of their fellow citizens. That's who they are - a bunch of thinly veiled wild animals.

FRESHIES LOVE TEARING EACH OTHER TO PIECES

In the face of a real disaster, their malice escalates to epic levels, as was demonstrated by Hurricane Katrina. Their top-level decision makers failed to authorize proper aid for the afflicted; police officers abandoned their positions to help their own families; and the victims of the storm themselves raped, murdered, and looted. Of course it's a hundred times worse than that now. People have broken off into small, isolated cells. Everyone wants to protect their own, and no one wants to run out of food, gas, or medical supplies, so they shoot at each other on a regular basis. Sometimes it seems like zombies are just bystanders - unblinking witnesses to humanity's self-immolation.

CROSSING SNAKE HANDS

JOURNAL ENTRIES

"WHOM SHALL I FEAR"

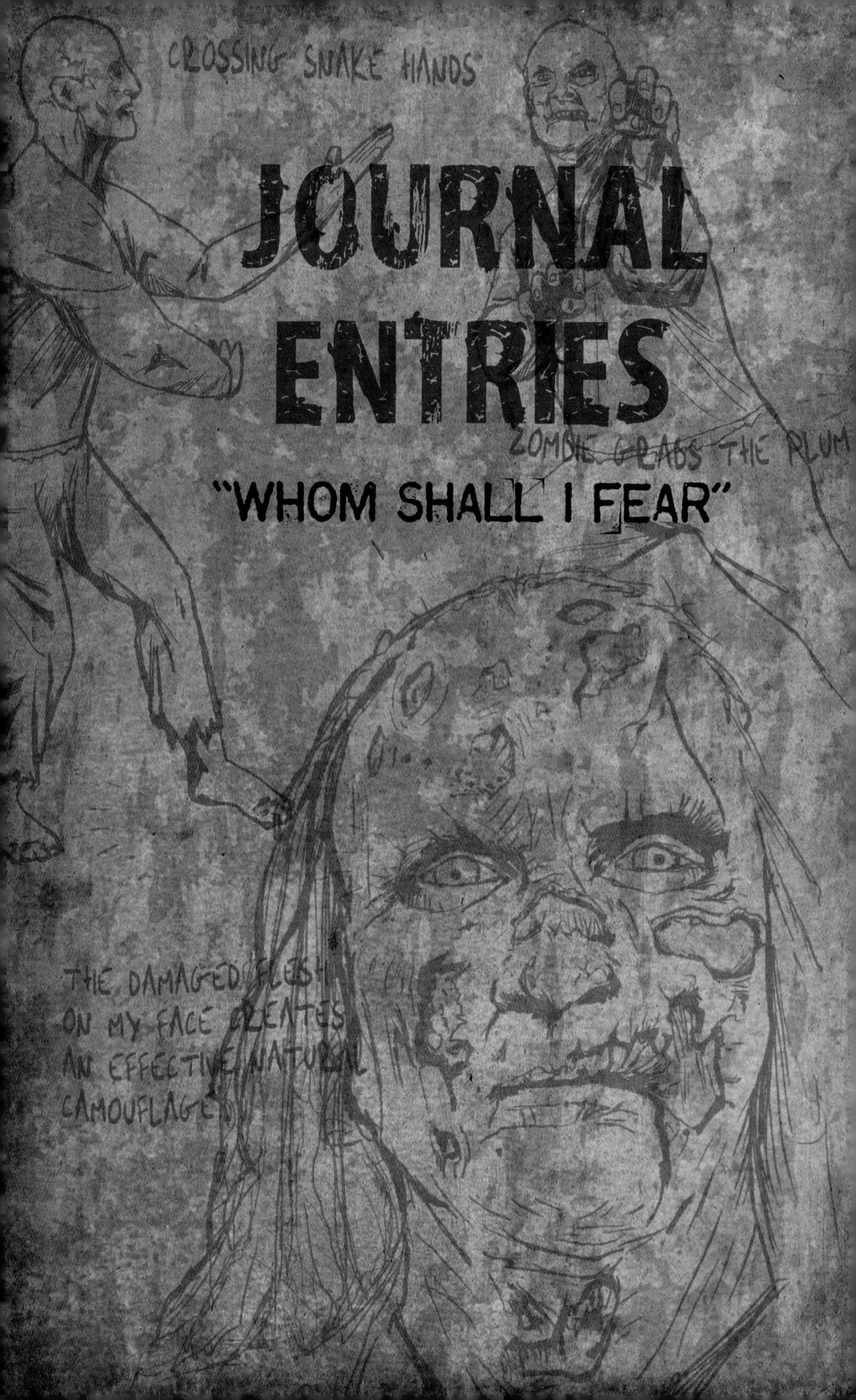

ZOMBIE GRABS THE PLUM

THE DAMAGED FLESH
ON MY FACE CREATES
AN EFFECTIVE NATURAL
CAMOUFLAGE

DAY 127 4:43 PM
THE RAIN OVER THE LAST FEW DAYS HAS GIVEN ME
A HEAVY FEELING. I'VE HAD THIS SENSATION BEFORE
WHEN IT'S RAINED, AND I ALWAYS THOUGHT IT WAS
DEPRESSION RELATED TO THE WEATHER. I FINALLY
FIGURED OUT IT'S JUST MY BODY GETTING WATER-
LOGGED. EVERY TIME IT RAINS, MY VESTIGIAL TISSUES
SOAK IT UP LIKE A SPONGE. I'LL BET I'M THIRTY
POUNDS HEAVIER RIGHT NOW THAN I WAS BEFORE THE
WEATHER CHANGED. MAYBE I'M A LITTLE DEPRESSED
TOO.

DAY 131 10:15 PM
ONE THING YOU HAVE TO GIVE TO THE FRESHIES
IS THAT THEY ARE SMART. NOW THAT THE DUST
HAS SETTLED ON THE OUTBREAK, THERE ARE SOME
ORGANIZED HUNTING PARTIES STARTING TO POP UP.
I JUST WATCHED FOUR GUYS IN A JEEP DO A "SHOOT
AND SCOOT" PROCEDURE WHERE THEY DROVE INTO
THE AREA, SOUNDED THE HORN, AND WAITED FOR THE
INFECTED TO START COMING. WHEN SLOW MOVERS
BEGAN TO ARRIVE, THE FRESHIES SAT THERE AND
PICKED THEM OFF BY THE DOZENS, ONLY TO SPEED
AWAY LIKE CHICKEN SHITS WHEN THE CROWD GOT A
LITTLE TOO THICK. I TRIED FOLLOWING THEM ON FOOT
TO SCORE SOME PAYBACK, BUT THEY HASTILY LEFT
THE AREA WHEN THE SUN STARTED GOING DOWN. I'M
SURE I WOULD SEE THIS KIND OF OPERATION EVERY DAY
IF MORE PEOPLE HAD CONFIDENCE IN THEIR SUPPLIES OF
AMMUNITION AND FUEL. IT'S A TROUBLING SIGN.

DAY 142 7:50 PM
I FOUND MYSELF LEAFING THROUGH MY JOURNAL TODAY,
REFRESHING MY MIND ON PAST LESSONS LEARNED.
THOUGH I ORIGINALLY STARTED TAKING NOTES AS A
MEANS OF CLARIFYING MY THOUGHTS, THIS JOURNAL
HAS SINCE GROWN INTO A POWERFUL EDUCATIONAL
RESOURCE. IT SEEMS LIKE A WASTE THAT I'M THE

ONLY ONE USING IT. THERE MUST BE SOMEONE ELSE
OUT THERE WHO SHARES MY STRANGE CONDITION.
WHATEVER MADE ME HOW I AM — BEING INFECTED, BUT
STILL ABLE TO THINK AND MOVE QUICKLY - CANNOT
HAVE HAPPENED ONLY TO ME AND HIPPIE GIRL. IT'S A
MATTER OF STATISTICS. EVEN IF IT OCCURS JUST ONE
TIME IN A MILLION, THAT WOULD MEAN THERE ARE FIFTY
OF US AT LEAST.

DAY 145 8:30 PM

THIS IS THE FIRST TIME SINCE MY SELF-IMPOSED FAST
THAT I HAVE GONE MORE THAN THREE DAYS WITHOUT
A KILL. IT'S MAKING ME ANTSY. YESTERDAY I ALMOST
BAGGED A MIDDLE-AGED LADY WHO WAS TENDING
TOMATO PLANTS IN A LOCAL CEMETERY (IT HAD GOOD
FENCES), BUT BEFORE I EVEN GOT CLOSE "BLAM-BA-
BLAM-BLAM-BLAM," HER REDNECK COHORTS LET FLY
WITH THE BULLETS. I HAD NO IDEA THOSE GUYS WERE
EVEN THERE. WERE THEY BAITING ME? THE WORLD IS
DEFINITELY GETTING TO BE A MORE DANGEROUS PLACE.
MAYBE IT'S BECAUSE ALL OF THE SOFT TARGETS
HAVE BEEN TAKEN OUT, LEAVING ONLY THE FRESHIES
WITH GUTS AND GUILE. OR MAYBE THE POCKETS OF
SURVIVORS HAVE, IN THEIR COLLECTIVE MIND, DECIDED TO
SET ASIDE THEIR DIFFERENCES AND JOIN FORCES TO WIPE
US OUT. I'M HOPING THE ANSWER TO THIS PROBLEM IS
AS SIMPLE AS A MOVE TO GREENER PASTURES.

DAY 169 7:18AM

I JUST WASTED MOTORCYCLE MAN. HE WAS PERCHED
ON A WATER TOWER WITH A COMMANDING VIEW OF THE
SUBURBS, SHARPSHOOTING SLOW MOVERS WITH HIS RIFLE.
HE PROBABLY FIGURED HE COULD SEE WELL ENOUGH TO
TIME AN ESCAPE IF TOO MANY ZOMBIES WERE GETTING
CLOSE. I CAN'T IMAGINE WHY HE WASN'T MORE
CAREFUL - HE HAD TO HAVE KNOWN I WAS OUT THERE
SOMEWHERE.

GETTING AT HIM WASN'T EASY. FIRST I HAD TO

HUNKER DOWN AND WATCH HIM WORK FOR A WHILE. IT MADE ME GRIND MY TEETH TO KNOW MY BROTHERS AND SISTERS WERE GETTING SHOT, BUT THIS GUY WAS GOOD, AND I KNEW I COULDN'T RUSH IT. AFTER ABOUT FORTY MINUTES, I SAW WHAT I WAS LOOKING FOR - A PATTERN. HE WOULD SHOOT FOR ABOUT FIVE MINUTES AND THEN WALK THE TOWER'S CATWALK WITH HIS BINOCULARS TO MAKE SURE HE STILL HAD A CLEAR ESCAPE. WHEN HIS CHECK WAS THROUGH, HE WOULD TAKE UP A NEW POSITION AND START SHOOTING AGAIN. AS SOON AS I FELT THE PREDICTABILITY OF HIS PROCEDURE, I CLOSED IN, ALWAYS MOVING WHILE HE WAS SHOOTING AND ALWAYS APPROACHING FROM HIS BLIND SIDE. THE CLIMB UP WAS THE MOST INTENSE PART SINCE I WOULD HAVE NOWHERE TO RUN IF HE SPOTTED ME ON THE LADDER. THOUGH MY ASCENT PROBABLY ONLY TOOK A FEW MINUTES, IT FELT LIKE AN ETERNITY. I MOVED SLOWLY AND DELIBERATELY UP EACH RUNG, MAKING A REAL EFFORT TO KEEP QUIET.

ONCE ON THE LANDING OF THE CATWALK, I JUDGED FROM THE REPORT OF HIS RIFLE THAT HE WAS JUST AROUND THE BEND FROM ME - IF I WAS AT THE TOWER'S SIX O'CLOCK POSITION, HE WAS AT ABOUT EIGHT OR NINE. I WAS SHITTING MY PANTS. IN SPITE OF THE COUNTLESS KILLS I'VE MADE OVER THE PAST FEW MONTHS, THIS GUY WAS ALWAYS KIND OF A BOOGEY MAN TO ME. I SUCKED IT UP, THOUGH, AND DID WHAT I KNEW I HAD TO DO - RUN RIGHT AT HIM AT FULL SPEED. HE HAD JUST STOOD UP WITH HIS BINOCULARS WHEN I HAMMERED HIM WITH WHAT THEY CALL IN FOOTBALL A "HELMET-TO-HELMET" HIT, IMPACTING HIS FACE WITH THE TOP OF MY HEAD. THE BLOW KNOCKED HIM UNCONSCIOUS IMMEDIATELY, ALMOST SENDING THE BOTH OF US RIGHT OVER THE RAILING. I'M SO OVERWHELMED WITH RELIEF. AS A REWARD FOR MY COURAGE, I NOW GET TO EAT HIS BRAINS WHILE ENJOYING A SCENIC VIEW.

MOVE YOUR HEAD

"Nothing in life is so exhilarating as to be shot at without result."

- Winston Churchill

A DEFENSIVE MANTRA

Though this chapter covers a wide variety of tools and techniques for self-preservation, I thought that "move your head" really captured it all in a nutshell. As I mentioned before, your E-node is your only real weakness, so when in doubt, move your head. Move it into cover, move it out of the way of deadly objects, and move it and the rest of your body the hell out of Dodge when you see that you're outmatched. Focus what seems like an inordinate amount of attention on your environment as it relates specifically to the position of your head. In this chapter are the practices that have kept me alive for so long against frightening odds.

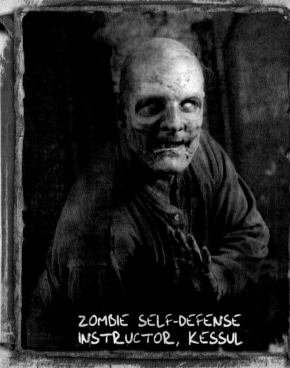

ZOMBIE SELF-DEFENSE
INSTRUCTOR, KESSUL

PROTECTIVE STANCES

When closing in on your opponent, you'll want to adopt a body position that prevents you from being brained or decapitated. Try to keep your chin tucked and shoulders slightly hunched to reduce the exposure of your neck, and keep your hands up to intercept blows directed at your head. When a weapon is coming at your head, there is no more certain protection for you than using your arms to block or parry. A block is simply putting your arms in between the blow and its intended target, so that they absorb the impact, while a parry is using your arms (or hands) to redirect the force of the blow, causing it to miss. Though the latter requires more skill, it will save your head with less risk of your suffering an arm amputation. Here are some protective stances recommended by Kessul, our zombie Sifu:

The Combat Box
With your arms in this position, enemy attacks from the side have no access to your head, and attacks from the top or front will be very easily picked off. This posture also serves to intimidate your opponent by making you

"THE COMBAT BOX"

seem larger, and it gives you a biomechenical advantage, putting gravity on your side when you drop your arms downward with a strike. You'll notice that a cat does the same thing in a fight, lifting its paw and holding it there so it is always poised to descend.

Long Bone Covers the Neck
The majority of your opponents will be right-handed, so holding your left arm in this bent position will block most of their swinging attacks, and cutting through your humeral (upper arm) bone longways will be almost

impossible for them, even with a robust weapon. Offensively, your bent arm is like a coiled spring, ready to fire your hand downward to rake your enemy's eyes or grab his hair or clothing.

Modified Cross Arm

With your chin tucked in the crook of your elbow, you make it very difficult for your enemy to get a clean shot at your head. Your elbow can easily be raised or lowered to ward off blows on any vector. Your extended arm acts not only as a grabbing weapon, but also as a defensive feeler that intercepts and redirects incoming attacks.

Peek-A-Boo

This is the boxing stance that Mike Tyson used to great effect while he was heavyweight champion. Clenched fists are not the best offensive weapons for zombies, but they will act as sturdy barriers to an enemy's strike.

"LONG BONE COVERS THE NECK"

"MODIFIED CROSS ARM"

"PEEK-A-BOO"

SELF-DEFENSE TECHNIQUES

I warned in Chapter 3 about the dangers of employing human martial arts, but when carefully adapted for use by zombies, ancient fighting systems can be highly effective. On the next several pages are a handful of techniques designed to protect you from freshie attacks. They are built around the free-flowing tai chi style, which is perfect for zombies - it makes you an elusive target and crowds your opponent, neutralizing his handheld weapons.

I would love to show you defenses for every type of weapon and every angle of attack, but it's better that you stick to just a few basics for now. Tackling too much too soon will only leave you overwhelmed. The freshie strikes I am going to cover are an excellent sampling of what you'll see in the real world and include the claw hammer, the pitchfork, and the screwdriver. Even when different weapons come into play, the swinging and thrusting motions your enemy uses will be much the same, so the same defensive techniques will still apply.

Study the defensive movements illustrated on the pages that follow, and spend hours rehearsing them with both your left and right hands (you have a lot of time in the day, so there is no excuse for failing to prepare). Keep practicing, and sooner or later you will find yourself in battle executing these life-saving maneuvers unconsciously.

THE FINISHING BITE

NOTE THAT ALL ZOMBIE SELF-DEFENSES END WITH A BITE, USUALLY TO THE ARM, SINCE GRABBING YOUR OPPONENT'S ARM IS THE KEY TO CONTROLLING HIS WEAPON. THIS IS THE POINT AT WHICH DEFENSE TURNS INTO OFFENSE. BITE AS HARD AS YOU CAN TO INSURE THAT YOUR TEETH GET THROUGH ALL LAYERS OF CLOTHING, SKIN, AND MUSCLE.

Figure 1
Start in the combat box position with your shoulders squared so either hand is ready for action. Though you'll appear flat-footed, your weight should be on the balls of your feet.

Figure 2
Stepping forward with your rear foot, slip your left hand under his shoulder and put your right hand on his wrist. This "push-pull" will give you excellent control of his weapon arm.

Figure 3
Collapse your body, bumping him with your hip. This will pull him off balance as you go in for the bite.

Pitchfork Thrust to the Body

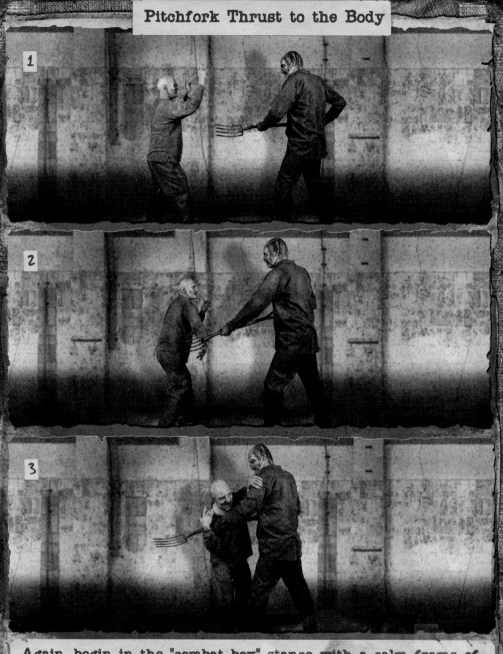

Again, begin in the "combat box" stance with a calm frame of mind (Figure 1). Step out with your left foot to clear your body of the target zone while checking the weapon with your right hand (Figure 2). Wrap your checking hand around the weapon, trapping your enemy's wrist between your forearm and shoulder, then finish with a bite to the radial artery (Figure 3).

With such a dangerous thrusting weapon so near to your head, you'll want to hold your arms slightly lower than with a typical combat box stance (Figure 1). Move your head out of the target zone while using your left hand to help you pass (Figure 2). Step in and do a "hand exchange" so that you're now checking the pitchfork with your right hand (Figure 3). Keep the pitchfork checked with your right hand and grab your opponent's lead foot pant leg with your left. With your enemy's weapon neutralized and his lower leg controlled, you are now in a position to bite to his femoral artery or groin (Figure 4).

Adopt a "wooden stance" to entice your enemy to attack (Figure 1). As his weapon comes forward, turn your torso to create space and bend ninety degrees at the waist (Figure 2a). Step in, rotate your torso forward, and explode upwards within the circumference of your enemy's arms. Push his chin to the side to expose his neck and bite his carotid artery (Figure 3a). Figure 2b shows a quick alternative: step in with your left foot, grabbing your opponent's wrist and shoulder for an immediate bite to the lower radial artery.

Figure 1
Hold your hands slightly wider apart to bait a strike to the center. This posture could also be used as a feigned surrender.

Figure 2
Suck your body in as he thrusts forward, and draw the screwdriver fully into your torso. This will cause your opponent to over-extend, pulling him off balance.

Figure 3
Make the top part of your body heavy, leaning your weight on the enemy's weapon arm as you continue to pull down and in. Bite repeatedly.

Screwdriver Thrust To The Head

Begin in the combat box stance (Figure 1). In the a-Series you "close the gate" by intercepting the weapon arm (Figure 2a), doing a hand exchange, and stuffing the arm as you go for the windpipe (Figure 3a). In the b-Series, you grab the weapon arm (Figure 2b) and loop it around to the outside for a jugular/carotid bite (Figure 3b).

FIGHTING MULTIPLE FOES

When you're alone and
facing more than one
opponent in a close-
quarters battle, the keys
to victory are crossing
the "T" and chaotic
movement.

THE SHIP ON THE
RIGHT CAN FIRE TWICE
AS MANY GUNS.

Crossing the "T" is an
expression derived
from naval combat that
describes positioning
your ship so that its side
faces the enemy's front.
This configuration allows
your ship to fire all
of its guns while the
enemy can only fire his few that face forward. It's about
maximizing your offensive capability while minimizing
that of your opponent. As a zombie facing a group in
combat, you'll want attack from a direction that "stacks"
your opponents, allowing only one of them to get to you
at a time. Whoever you are attacking, always keep that
target in between yourself and the rest of the group. As
the battle unfolds, continue moving to keep your enemies
stacked.

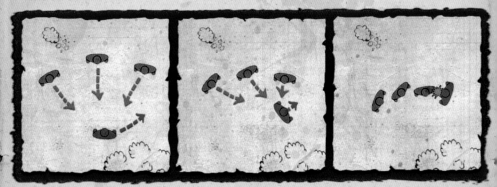

If you find yourself in the middle of a mob where crossing
the "T" is not possible, use chaotic movement as a defense.
Aggressively grab the closest target and roll with your
victim like an alligator as you work him over with your
bite, or spin with him if you are both still on your feet.
This will make it impossible for the other freshies in the
fight to take a clean shot at you. Don't spend more than a

few seconds getting your licks in before leaping for your next victim (even if your first victim isn't dead yet, he's probably out of the fight). Repeat the biting and rolling with your second and subsequent victims.

Whichever technique you use, you'll find when you've taken out two freshies in a row, the rest usually don't stick around for their turn. Though it sounds awesome bursting into a room full of guys, killing a couple, and watching the rest run away, I don't recommend that beginners take on large groups of opponents by themselves. Having a real veteran's sense of battle is critical to the split-second decision-making necessary to win.

ZOMBIE HEADGEAR

I generally espouse a philosophy of traveling light when it comes to zombie equipment, but wearing a helmet is always, always worth the hassle. Any helmet is better than none, even if it means wearing one of those fruity bike helmets into battle. It will more than double the protection already provided by your skull. The two variables you need to consider when choosing a helmet are coverage and protective value.

ME IN A CATCHER'S MASK, FIELD MODIFIED FOR BITING

Coverage
The more area of your head and neck that is protected, the better. A football or motorcycle helmet would each give great coverage, protecting the back and sides of your head completely. Their facial coverage is a bonus as well, but you'll have to alter the face mask to enable you to bite. Don't forget that you can cover your nose completely with your helmet modifications - you're no longer a breather.

Protective Value
Most sports helmets are similar in their resistance to blows, and all make it difficult for an enemy to damage

THIS "STEEL POT" HELMET WILL STOP SOME BULLETS

A HIGHLY EFFECTIVE MODEL FOR HAND-TO-HAND COMBAT

your E-node with a handheld weapon. In addition to being shock and penetration resistant, sports helmets provide glancing surfaces, causing blows to be deflected away; but be mindful that they provide almost no ballistic protection, meaning that your vulnerability to bullets will be largely unchanged. If you have a sports helmet, you might want to beef up its protective value with some sheet metal or other bits of added armor. Military helmets were designed to resist high-velocity shrapnel and some pistol ammunition, so a steel or especially Kevlar helmet is your best bet. A Kevlar helmet will bounce everything from .22 caliber rounds to .45 ACP and 9mm hollowpoints, making it a lifesaver for sure.

Since zombies are hand-to-hand fighters, you'll want to make sure your helmet is securely fastened at all times. Chin straps are an obvious answer to this problem, though I always feel like they constrain my jaw a little when it comes to biting. If you really want your helmet to stay put, I recommend screwing it to your head. Measure the thickness of your helmet carefully, including any padding, lining, or airspace, and choose a screw length that will cover that distance plus 1/2" to 3/4". The latter numbers represent the depth that the screws will penetrate into your skull. Four to eight screws will do the job fine - that helmet won't be going anywhere. Any more than eight screws will only compromise the structure of your skull with an undue number of holes. Driving screws into your head without help is quite a challenge and will require a power drill, a mirror, and a lot of patience.

SERPENTINING

"Serpentining" is a means of frustrating a shooter's aim by running in a zig-zag pattern when moving over open ground. There is some argument as to whether this is effective or just silly. I usually use a compromise technique, making periodic cuts like a running back, as opposed to doing the full-blown zig-zag. It's worked for me so far. Varying your running speed also helps, as it makes it difficult for a sniper to time his shot. Even more important than evasive movement, perhaps, is to make sure you have IDed a safe destination before starting your run.

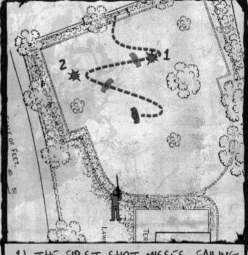

1) THE FIRST SHOT MISSES, FAILING TO LEAD THE RUNNING TARGET.
2) THE NEXT SHOT LEADS THE TARGET, BUT DOESN'T ANTICPATE ITS SUDDEN CHANGE IN DIRECTION.

Otherwise, you may find yourself dashing all the way back to your starting point to find refuge from enemy fire.

THE INVISIBLE HUNTER

Seeing your enemy before he sees you gives you the initiative, allowing you to choose the manner and direction of your attack. Even more important, it allows you to choose not to attack when the odds aren't in your favor. Here are some rules you should always follow in order to keep yourself unnoticed.

Use Camouflage

Camouflage is about blending in with your surroundings and breaking up the distinctive body shapes that the human eye is genetically programmed to identify. To this end, consider among other things your clothing, body coloration, and reflectivity.

1) Clothing - If you are wearing civilian attire with fairly neutral colors, all of the seepage from your body and grime from everyday life will soon turn your clothes into an excellent, earthy camouflage. Pre-outbreak homeless people were excellent examples of this - with their dingy apparel, those guys would practically disappear when crouched against a building. Tattered sleeves and pant legs are also a bonus since the way that they drape helps to mask your humanoid form. If you are wearing bright colors or unnatural patterns (plaid, for instance), I would recommend changing. Otherwise, just let nature take care of your defensive coloration. Trust me when I say there's no need to go overboard with military or

hunting fabrics. Since you are no longer doing laundry, their camouflage patterns will eventually be muted down to nothing by grime anyway.

2) Body Coloration - Using camouflage paint may be a good idea, but the PACE infection is once again a good provider here. Your sores, wounds and skin discolorations break up your human-like features, making your face harder to recognize as distinct from your background. If you do use face paint, follow the old rules of using dark colors on the high areas (chin, nose, ears, cheekbones, and forehead), and light colors on sunken areas (eye sockets). And there's definitely no need to look for military-grade greasepaint. Your skin has no sensitivity to chemicals, so you can even use latex house paint if you want to.

3) Reflectivity - Make sure you aren't wearing jewelry or other objects that reflect light. If your skin or wounds are slimy, dull the shine with dry dirt or powder of some kind.

Don't Silhouette Yourself
The idea here is to position yourself so that your background doesn't contrast starkly with the shape of your body. Standing on top of a hill with nothing but the sunny sky behind you is an extreme example of silhouetting yourself (military types refer to this as "skylining"). To avoid this problem, the main thing you want to do is keep your body low. If you want to see on the other side of a half-wall, peek around it instead of popping your head up over the top. Going under a fence is always better than going over it, and if you're going over it, lay on it and slide over instead of hopping it.

Observe Noise Discipline
You want to be a ghost when it comes to creeping up on freshies silently, so turn off any chimes or alarms if you're wearing a watch and secure anything on your body that will clank or rattle. This is usually unnecessary advice for a zombie since we're not big on keys and jewelry, but the importance of the idea still stands. If you're like me, your body has some of its own little noises; in my case it's a popping right knee. The knee works fine, mind you, but there's something going on with the vestigial tissue that's making noise when I put weight on it, and cutting the tendons in that area didn't seem to help. I can control the

noise of it when I try (by walking a little stiff-legged), but the trick knee will keep me from ever being a superstar of the quiet approach.

Mind Your Scent
People trained in reconnaissance are taught to smell the air for traces of their enemy - odors such as cigarette smoke, cooked rations, or vehicle exhaust. With us it will be zombie stink they are sniffing for. I mentioned previously how Febreze can help, but there is not much else you can do besides staying downwind of anyone you want to evade (that means the wind should be blowing from the direction of your enemy toward you). Remember that you can't smell anything now other than human brains, so you have no way of knowing what your odor is or how strong it might be.

THE ELUSIVE TRAVELER

Your quest for brains will have you criss-crossing the countryside, and if astute freshies become aware of you, they can use your movement habits as a tool in hunting you. Here is a list of important safety guidelines regarding the time, place, and manner of your travel.

Be a Minimalist
I follow the rule of the old-school Harley crowd: If it doesn't fit in your pockets, leave it behind. In addition to carrying the pouch with my journal and camera, I'll usually carry one or two things in each front pants pocket - maybe a lighter, a pen, or a pocket knife - but that's it. And I don't get attached to any of

MY TRUSTY JOURNAL POUCH

that stuff. One of the most incredible aspects of this new life is that you are completely self-sufficient without having possessions. As soon as you start getting attached to things, you can get bogged down very quickly. The process is insidious - first you need a few things; then you need a fanny pack; then you need a backpack; then you need a place to store the stuff you can't carry with you;

I'LL PROBABLY HANG ON TO THIS LIGHTER UNTIL IT RUNS OUT OF FUEL.

then, before you know it, you're geographically anchored to one spot, becoming a hunter with limited range who can be tracked back to his habitual hideout.

Keep Moving
Someday you may stumble onto an excellent hunting ground where brains are plentiful and easily obtained. Even so, know that you can't stick around too long. You have to be disciplined when it comes to moving on. No matter how safe you feel, if you make a habit of lingering in one area of operation, sooner or later someone will get wise and smoke you. The lazy mistake of going too often to the same well has been the undoing of countless master criminals who, now in prison, might otherwise be lounging at a beach resort in Bali.

Keep It Irregular
As soon as someone can anticipate your comings and goings, you're dead in the water, so don't fall into any patterns of behavior. Always vary your routes and the times that you use them.

Move at Night
A sniper with a scoped rifle can be deadly out to a thousand yards during the day. Without night vision optics, that deadly range drops to a few hundred yards or less in the dark. Since long-range fighting is the enemy's game, operate at night as often as possible to take his best capability away from him.

Don't Drive

With showrooms full of vehicles there for the taking, it may cross your mind to drive as a means of travel. But don't succumb to the temptation. You can run at about 15mph indefinitely and can use terrain features along with your super stamina to evade almost any pursuer. In a car you lose that advantage. If you are behind the wheel, and freshies roll up on you in a car of their own and start firing, you're in big trouble. In a car, where you go, they can go, and they will likely have both a driver and gunners. Vehicles, with their noise, visibility, and predictable routes of travel, draw entirely too much attention for a smart zombie to want to use them.

STOP, LOOK, LISTEN, SMELL

Freshies are always on the lookout for you, and you should be on the lookout for them as well. When you're on the move, it's good every once in a while to find concealment, sit very still and take in your surroundings. Can you see movement, hear a distant vehicle, or smell brains? It's amazing what you can perceive when you quiet yourself and focus. Remember, too, that you need 360 degree awareness. "Keep your head on a swivel," as they say in the Spec Ops community, looking left, right, and behind you.

DESTROY CAPTURED ASSETS

Once you've dispatched an enemy, check his equipment to make sure there is nothing of use in it for other freshies who come along. Anything you find that may be helpful to them should be destroyed.

Ammunition

This is a little tricky, but it must be taken care of diligently. What I've been doing is taking ammo out of its boxes and magazines and throwing it into deep bodies of water, like rivers or ponds. A well or septic tank will also do. It crossed my mind to just load the bullets

JUST A FEW HANDFULS CAN KILL DOZENS OF ZOMBIES

and shoot them all off, but that would be time consuming, and sustained, rhythmic gunfire would draw too much attention. Burning ammo is not advisable either, since slow movers tend to flock to the source of any man-made noise, and you don't want your fellow zombies gathering around a fire with hundreds of rounds of ammunition cooking off.

Weapons
Dismantle firearms, breaking and dispersing their component parts. Bend their barrels and smash their receivers.

Rations
Dump food out of its packages and mix it with chemicals, feces, or other despoiling agents.

Medicine
Treat medical supplies as you would food, dumping them out and mixing them with unwholesome things. If you find any large syringes, take them and keep them in their sterile packages. I'll explain their usefulness in Chapter 6.

A WALL-MOUNTED BOX LIKE THIS CAN'T BE LEFT INTACT

Vehicles
Burn vehicles, or, at a minimum, slash their tires, cut their engine wires, and puncture their fluid reservoirs. Make sure any surplus fuel containers are emptied.

Miscellaneous Gear
There are all kinds of things that can make a freshie's post-apocalyptic life safer and more comfortable. Use your best judgment in deciding whether or not a particular item is worth sticking around to destroy. Definitely disable prized equipment (like a generator, for instance), but taking the time to destroy lesser gear (like winter clothing) will be a more questionable call.

I know it's a drag going through all of the effort to "scorch the earth" this way, but it's critical to your survival. There are no longer any factories making new weapons, ammunition and equipment for the freshies, so anything you take out of circulation will not be replaced. As you make the enemy's resources increasingly scarce, the less of a threat he will become, and the more he will have to leave his fortifications to seek out supplies.

LEAVE NO WITNESSES

The fact that people aren't expecting zombies to be smart and fast gives you the advantage of surprise in almost every situation. As soon as it becomes general knowledge that our kind exist, that advantage will evaporate. You can never kill every witness - someone always gets away - but kill as many as you can so word of your existence will spread more slowly.

THERE WAS GRASS BELOW
BUT FALLING FROM THIS
HEIGHT STILL COULD HAVE
KILLED ME.

JOURNAL
ENTRIES

"SELF-KNOWLEDGE"

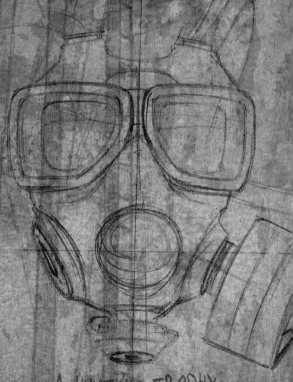

A HUNTING TROPHY
ALMOST WORTH KEEPING.

DAY 169 8:12 AM
HOLY SHIT. HOLY SHIT!!! GOING THROUGH MOTORCYCLE
MAN'S GEAR, I FOUND A ROAD MAP OF THE CITY WITH
A DIRTY FINGERPRINT INDICATING HIS PROBABLE BASE
OF OPERATIONS. AND THAT'S NOT EVEN THE GOOD
PART. WHILE MONITORING HIS WALKIE-TALKIE, I HEARD
REFERENCES TO A "DR. NOVAK." ACCORDING TO MY OLD
NOTES, THERE WAS A DR. NOVAK ON THE PACE VIRUS
RESEARCH TEAM. I GAVE UP ON FINDING ANY OF THOSE
ASSHOLES A LONG TIME AGO, BUT EVERYTHING HAPPENS
FOR A REASON. I'M A SEASONED KILLER NOW WITH
THE STRENGTH OF FOUR MEN. I'VE NEVER BEEN IN A
BETTER POSITION TO GO AFTER THEM.

DAY 169 9:00 AM
I JUST MADE THE THREE-MILE HUMP TO THE
INTERSECTION THAT WAS UNINTENTIONALLY MARKED ON
THE MAP. TIME TO SIT STILL, WATCH, AND WAIT.

DAY 169 4:30 PM
OKAY, I'VE IDENTIFIED THE LOCATION IN QUESTION - A FIVE-
STORY BRICK INDUSTRIAL BUILDING WHERE AMBULANCES
USED TO BE MANUFACTURED. THE FRESHIES CHOSE
WELL. IT HAS STOUT DOORS, HIGH WINDOWS, AND A
MASSIVE VEHICLE ELEVATOR TO CARRY THEM AND THEIR
EQUIPMENT SAFELY UP AND DOWN. THERE ISN'T MUCH
ELSE IN THE WAY OF SECURITY, THOUGH. A LOOKOUT IS
WATCHING FROM A FRONT WINDOW ON THE THIRD FLOOR,
PROBABLY WAITING FOR MOTORCYCLE MAN TO COME
BACK. THE ABSENCE OF SLOW MOVERS IN THE AREA IS
CREEPING ME OUT. NOT A FRIENDLY NEIGHBORHOOD.

THE PROBLEM NOW IS HOW TO GET IN THERE. I
CONSIDERED DOING WHAT I SWORE I'D NEVER DO AGAIN
AND TRY TO PASS MYSELF OFF AS A FRESHIE. WEARING
MOTORCYCLE MAN'S CLOTHES AND GAS MASK, I MIGHT BE
ABLE TO ROLL RIGHT IN THE FRONT DOOR, BUT I DON'T
KNOW WHAT THEIR PASSWORD PROTOCOL IS. I CAN'T BE
POSITIVE THIS GROUP EVEN KNOWS MOTORCYCLE MAN.

DAY 169 6:10 PM
THE FIRE ESCAPE ON THE BACK OF THE BUILDING HAS
BEEN CUT WITH A TORCH TO ABOUT TWELVE FEET
ABOVE THE GROUND. I THINK THAT'S THE TICKET. IF I
COULD GET A LADDER UNDER IT, I'D PRETTY MUCH BE IN.
I'LL PROBABLY JUST FIND A SIX-FOOTER, CARRY IT OVER
ON MY BACK, STAND ON THE TOP OF IT, AND REACH UP.

DAY 170 1:45 AM
WHERE DO I BEGIN? MY BELLY IS SO FULL OF BRAINS
I WISH I COULD TAKE A NAP. I'LL BE PUKING UP
WASTE PELLETS FOR DAYS. I DIDN'T END UP NEEDING
A LADDER TO GET IN; AN OVERTURNED 55-GALLON
DRUM GAVE ME PLENTY OF HEIGHT TO JUMP UP TO
THE FIRE ESCAPE (MY VERTICAL LEAP IS SICK WITH
ALL OF THIS NEW STRENGTH). I WAS EXPECTING
THIS PLACE TO BE AN IMPREGNABLE SUPERFORTRESS,
BUT ONCE I GOT TO AN ENTRANCE, THE TAKEDOWN
WAS NO BIG DEAL - JUST A TYPICAL FRESHIE NEST. I
MADE SHORT WORK OF THEIR HACK "SECURITY" GUYS,
THEN TRACKED DOWN THE OTHERS ONE BY ONE WHEN
THEY SCATTERED. NOVAK, HIS TWO KIDS, A HANDFUL OF
ARMED FLUNKIES - A TOTAL OF EIGHT PEOPLE IF I'M NOT
MISTAKEN. I HAD TO BREAK DOWN A STOUT FIRE DOOR
TO FINALLY GET AT THE MAN HIMSELF. I WAS LICKING
MY CHOPS. IN A PERFECT WORLD HE WOULD HAVE
APOLOGIZED AND BEGGED FOR MERCY, BUT THIS AIN'T
A PERFECT WORLD. NOVAK WAS A COLD, DISCONNECTED
PIECE OF SHIT, EVEN WHEN I THREATENED THE LIVES
OF HIS GIRLS. HE DID EXPLAIN WHAT HAPPENED TO ME,
THOUGH, AND I'M GRATEFUL FOR THAT.

IT SEEMS I WAS NO ANGEL IN MY PRE-INFECTION LIFE.
MY JOB AT THE LAB WAS TO TAKE HUMAN REMAINS
NO LONGER USEFUL FOR RESEARCH AND DISSOLVE
THEM WITH ACID, THUS DESTROYING EVIDENCE OF THE
COMPANY'S PRACTICES. THERE IS NO DOING A JOB LIKE
THAT WITHOUT KNOWING IT'S WRONG. I THREATENED
TO BLOW THE WHISTLE ON THE WHOLE PROJECT,

THOUGH, WHEN THEY BROUGHT IN ISABELLE, MY HIPPIE PRINCESS. SHE WAS A DRUG ADDICT THEY COAXED INTO THE LAB, PROMISING HER CASH TO BE PART OF A "PHARMACEUTICAL TRIAL." WHEN I VOICED MY OBJECTIONS, THEY TASED AND SEDATED ME AND STRAPPED ME ONTO A GURNEY BED NEXT TO ISABELLE AND SOME GUY NAMED "RON." THEN THEY INFECTED ALL THREE OF US BY INJECTING THE VIRUS DIRECTLY INTO OUR BRAIN STEMS.

THAT'S WHY WE'RE DIFFERENT. SINCE THE VIRUS TOOK OVER OUR BRAIN STEMS FIRST, IT WAS ABLE TO BUILD A ZOMBIE FROM A LIVE BODY, COMMANDEERING VITAL CORTICAL TISSUE AND PRESERVING MANY SYNAPTIC CONNECTIONS. THINGS WENT TO HELL IN A BUCKET AT THE LAB WHEN THEY STARTED FEEDING FRESH HUMAN BRAIN TISSUE TO RON IN ORDER TO STUDY ITS EFFECTS. HE WAS APPARENTLY PRETTY HUSKY AS IT WAS, AND THE ADDITION OF BRAIN-EATER STRENGTH PUT HIM OVER THE TOP, ALLOWING HIM TO SNAP HIS RESTRAINTS AND START WRECKING THE PLACE. HE LET ISABELLE LOOSE AND UNDID MY STRAPS, EVEN THOUGH I HAD BEEN INJECTED LAST AND WAS STILL UNCONSCIOUS. IT WAS ON - THE BIRTH OF A ZOMBIE APOCALYPSE. I WISH I KNEW WHAT BECAME OF BIG RON. IN MY EYES HE WILL ALWAYS BE "PATIENT ZERO," THE FIRST OF US TO BREAK FREE AND GO TO WAR.

NOW KNOWING ALL OF THAT, I PUZZLED OVER WHAT TO DO WITH NOVAK. I THOUGHT ABOUT TYING HIM TO A CHAIR, BITING HIS BIG TOE, AND WATCHING THE INFECTION TAKE OVER HIS BODY INCH BY INCH. I ALSO CONSIDERED INFECTING HIS DAUGHTERS AND LETTING THEM EAT HIM, BUT THAT WOULD BE SICK. IN THE END I JUST KNOCKED HIS HEAD OPEN AND ATE HIS BRAIN. THAT WAS THE CLOSEST THING TO JUSTICE I COULD THINK OF - TO DO BATTLE WITH AN OLD DEMON, CONSUME HIM, AND BE NOURISHED BY HIM. NOW I'M ON TO A BIGGER PIECE OF BUSINESS... BUILDING AN ARMY.

CHAPTER 6

INFECT OTHERS

"He who fights with monsters might take care lest he thereby become a monster."

- Friedrich Nietsche

THE FOUR I's

We, as a species, are at war, fighting for the brain-eating lifestyle to which we are entitled. Winning this war will mean thinking strategically and sometimes suspending our immediate want for brains in order to create more zombies. We must grow our ranks to put our enemy on the defensive, where he belongs, so that he may be hunted and harvested without threatening our way of life. And _you_ must do your part. Creating a proper zombie army is a multistep process that will require discipline and technique, and remembering the steps is a matter of knowing your four I's: Ingest, Infect, Inject, and Instruct.

INGEST

Ingesting brains is necessary to keep you healthy and well. Yes, there is a mighty cause that calls you, but as I detailed in Chapter 1, failure to eat brains can make an intelligent zombie lose his mind, and this is something we cannot afford. Always be sure your own dietary needs are met before moving on to the "infection" portion of the manifesto. It's the same principle as a flight attendant telling you to put on your own oxygen mask before putting on your child's - you won't be able to help anyone else if you haven't first taken care of yourself. Make it a priority to eat at least one brain a week to keep your mind sound; eat two or more if you are in an area where prey is scarce.

INFECT

Slow-moving zombies are like the worker ants to our warriors and queens - their business is not as glamorous as ours, but they are essential to the operation of our system. A huge, eternally patrolling army of slow movers puts the freshies in a mindset of survival, as opposed to one of offense, allowing us to travel in the shadows and strike deliberately. To create a slow mover, you need only bite a victim and then let him go. That's easier said than done, of course, since your feeding instinct will be in overdrive that close to live prey, but you'll be surprised at your own willpower, especially if you've kept up on your feeding. When intending only to infect, the best places to bite your

SEARCH AND DESTROY

MUCH LIKE ANTS, SLOW-MOVING ZOMBIES HUNT BY WANDERING. THEY MEANDER AROUND, CHANGING DIRECTION ACCORDING TO SOME KIND OF INTERNAL ALGORITHM UNTIL THEIR SENSES PICK UP A TRACE OF FOOD. THIS TIRELESS EXPLORATION WILL CARRY THEM TO EVERY NOOK AND CRANNY OF THE LANDSCAPE, LEAVING THE FRESHIES NO PLACE TO HIDE.

enemy are the head, neck, shoulders, and torso. Zombie bite wounds to these areas will position the virus to kill in 5-30 minutes and allow no possibility of halting the infection via amputation.

Infecting from a Distance

If you don't mind carrying a little gear - something you must be wary of - you can infect freshies at ranges of up to 100 yards or more. The optimum tool for this, in my experience, is a high-powered .177 caliber air rifle loaded with the pointed variety of hunting pellets. Such a weapon is relatively light and quiet; it requires little cleaning, and its ammunition weighs almost nothing - you can carry thousands of pellets without being encumbered. The bad thing, though, is that loading the tiny pellets one at a time is quite an exercise with clumsy zombie fingers.

Use of the air rifle is pretty simple: when approching prey, just put a small handful of pellets in your mouth to get them virus-rich, then load and fire them at the enemy body parts I just mentioned. They should break the skin with no problem, unless you are at extended range or your enemy is wearing protective clothing. For those of you who are wondering, infection by projectile is not possible using firearms. The high temperatures created in the barrel by the burning gunpowder will kill any viral material you put on a bullet.

NOTE: In Chapter 3 I went on at some length about the foolishness of shooting it out with freshies, and that admonition stands. Using an air rifle to infect is for "advanced students" only. If you're thinking about trying it but are not sure if you're ready, then you're not ready.

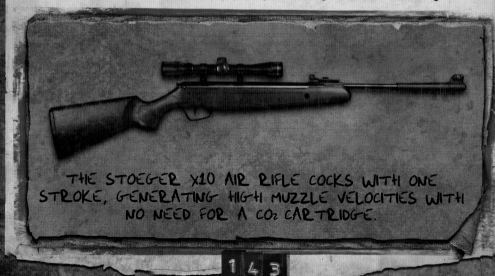

THE STOEGER X10 AIR RIFLE COCKS WITH ONE STROKE, GENERATING HIGH MUZZLE VELOCITIES WITH NO NEED FOR A CO₂ CARTRIDGE.

INJECT

There is no more precious gift you can give to zombiekind than bringing another sharp, self-aware sibling into our family. In doing so, you are effectively doubling yourself for the purposes of our war, fielding a fighter who, on his own, can disrupt many square miles of enemy-held territory. And let's not forget the favor you are doing for your victim - replacing his fear with clarity and relative immortality. Seeding a fast-mover is a fragile, almost surgical procedure, and the things that can go wrong with it are many. What makes it complicated is that you must introduce the infection into the victim's brain stem without the virus touching any intervening tissues. If the virus gets into the muscle or bone, it will rip through the victim's head, killing vital brain matter long before the E-node is established, and the result will be a slow mover. I have created a lot of slow movers with botched injection attempts, failing to take enough care in having the virus enter the brain stem first. It makes for a frustrating feeling, especially considering how difficult it is to secure a live freshie for injection.

The Process
If you want to attempt a seeding, the first thing you'll need to do is gather the following items or their equivalents: duct tape, a cup or glass, a large syringe, alcohol or iodine, and latex or vinyl gloves. You may want to keep some of these things on your person as a matter of habit since they are all pretty small and light, and you never know when a good opportunity to seed will present itself. Once you are properly equipped, follow this checkilst in order:

A TYPICAL BRAIN STEM INJECTION KIT

1) **Locate a Victim** - Find a lone freshie - either one who is by himself to begin with, or one whose friends you have already taken out.

2) **Immobilize Him** - Subdue him (usually by beating or choking) and bind him hand and foot with duct tape, zip ties, or whatever is handy.

"HOG TIE"

A GREAT WAY TO RESTRAIN YOUR VICTIM'S MOVEMENT

3) **Mix Your Solution** - Put about two ounces of water into a glass and take some of it into your mouth. Swish it around for a few seconds and spit it back into the glass. The water is now swimming with the PACE virus.

4) **Sterilize Your Hands** - Put on a pair of rubber gloves and sterilize them with alcohol so you can keep your intruments free of the virus.

5) **Ready the Needle** - Dip the needle of your syringe into the glass and draw a few CCs of the infected water into it. Sterilize the exterior of the needle with alcohol to make sure there is no living PACE virus on its surface.

6) **Assume the Position** - Roll your victim onto his belly and sit on his upper back.

7) **Inject** - Insert the needle into the base of the skull, putting it through the foramen magnum - the large hole where the spinal cord enters - at a steep, upward angle. Push it gently and jimmy it around a little to make sure it's not hung up on anything hard. Keep pushing until it's 1 1/2 or more inches deep below the skin. Only when the needle is perfectly seated should you push the plunger, injecting the infection directly into the brain

stem. **DO NOT REMOVE THE NEEDLE** or you will drag the infected tip through the victim's neck tissue.

8) Wait for Results - Relax and wait about two hours for reanimation.

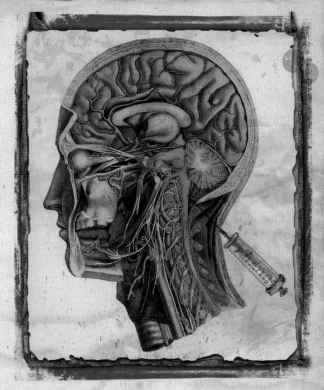

You'll know that you have succeeded if your infected victim bolts to life suddenly as if he's just been doused with ice water. Only fast movers reanimate this way, and it's a beautiful sight - enough to bring seepage to your eyes. But a failed seedling will drag himself around sluggishly - a slow-moving consolation prize for your lack of technique.

Candidates for Injection

As you can see, turning someone into a fast mover is no easy task, so you want to make sure you have chosen a good host for the virus before going to such great lengths to inject him. The quandary we face is that we want tough, smart recruits, but it's hard to subdue tough, smart freshies. Abducting people who are stupid or unskilled in combat is the path of least resistance in the short run, but then what kind of army would we have? The ideal solution, I believe, is to target people who are physically enfeebled but are warriors at heart. In my experience, disabled veterans of foreign wars are ideal candidates, especially if they are in a wheelchair, walk with a cane, or are bed-ridden. Once infected, these lionhearted men regain full use of their bodies and fight like pit bulls let off the chain. Kessul was a great example of this. Put in a wheelchair by a roadside bomb, he used the strength of the virus to rise and fight again in glory.

INSTRUCT

After successfully making a clean brainstem injection, your next order of business is to indoctrinate the newly reanimated fast mover. It is a huge responsiblity being the first face someone sees when they enter the world - empathy is key here. Remember how disoriented and dismayed you were in your first moments as a zombie. Before jumping into intellectual matters like zombie anatomy and ambush tactics, you must first make this newborn brother emotionally at ease. If you can, keep a captured freshie nearby so that you can quickly give the seedling his first feed. Eating a fresh human brain will help snap everything into perspective for him. While he is experiencing the high of having consumed his first brain, ease him into an understanding of what has happened and what he has become. The more brains he eats in the first few hours of reanimation, the more easily he will accept his new existence.

Once he has settled in a bit, give him a copy of "The Brain Eater's Bible" and review it with him. Help him to understand that he is not a monster, that he is beautiful, and that his carnivorous instincts support a just cause. Take him into the field and teach him until you feel he gets it on an intellectual and spiritual level. This process could take as little as a few days or as long as a few months, but you must eventually release him into the world on his own. His purpose now is to travel far, siring new zombies and bringing the fight to another territory. Fortunately for us, the principles by which we live are sound and in perfect alignment with all of our natural instincts. The chances are good that your creation, that new branch on the zombie tree of life, will flourish as a lone hunter.

OUR FAMILY TREE IS GNARLED AND GROWS LIKE A WEED

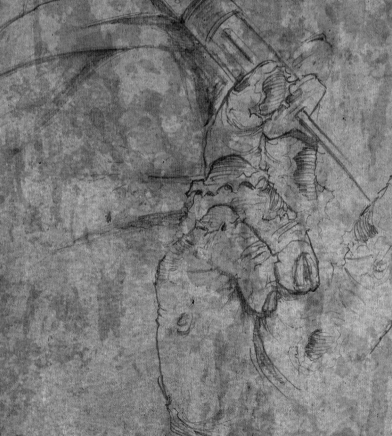

JOURNAL ENTRIES

"MY BROTHER'S MAKER"

DAY 198 2:15 AM
I HAVE ONLY A FEW PAGES LEFT IN THIS JOURNAL
AND SO MUCH TO TELL. THE TIDE IS TURNING IN OUR
FAVOR. OUR NEW RECRUITS ARE WICKED FIGHTERS,
AND I AM GIVING EACH OF THEM A COPY OF MY COMPILED
RESEARCH - A WORK WHICH I AM CALLING "THE BRAIN
EATER'S BIBLE."

MY PRIZE SEEDLING IS LUCINDA, A TWENTY YEAR-OLD
FORMER FREE RUNNING CHAMPION WHO ALREADY HAS
OVER FORTY KILLS. THE GIRL IS LIKE SPIDERMAN THE
WAY SHE CLIMBS, JUMPS, AND ROLLS; THERE DOESN'T
SEEM TO BE A PHYSICAL BARRIER THAT CAN STOP HER.
LAST WEEK I EQUIPPED HER WITH A KEVLAR HELMET
AND A PAIR OF ICE PICKS AND SICKED HER ON A SMALL
MILITARY COMPOUND. AFTER SCRAMBLING OVER THE
CHAIN LINK FENCE LIKE IT WAS HORIZONTAL, SHE GOT
INSIDE AND INFECTED EVERYONE IN SIGHT. CONTINUALLY
LICKING THE POINTS OF HER WEAPONS, SHE RAN UP ON
FRESHIES AND THRUST THE INFECTION RIGHT THROUGH
THEIR BODY ARMOR. THOUSANDS OF ROUNDS WERE
FIRED AT HER, BUT SHE WAS TOO DAMNED ELUSIVE FOR
ANYONE TO MANAGE A HEADSHOT. WHEN THE ENEMY
STARTED TO PANIC IT TURNED INTO A ROUTE, AND
THAT DAY DOZENS OF DEADLY FOES BECAME SLOW-MOVING
PAWNS ON OUR SIDE OF THE BOARD.

ANOTHER HERO AMONG THE NEWLY INFECTED IS
JEREMIAH, AN ELDERLY, RETIRED IRONWORKER. HE HAS
BEEN ABLE TO FABRICATE AMAZING FULL-COVERAGE HEAD
ARMOR FOR OUR ELITE FAST MOVERS. MADE OF THICK,
FACE-HARDENED STEEL, HIS CUSTOM HELMETS STOP
EVEN LIGHT RIFLE ROUNDS. ONLY OUR STURDIER GUYS
CAN WEAR THEM DUE TO THE NECK STRENGTH THEY
REQUIRE, BUT A ZOMBIE SO PROTECTED IS ALL BUT
INVINCIBLE. NED KELLY WOULD BE PROUD.

I MUST ENJOY THIS WHILE I CAN, FOR THESE ARE SURELY THE HALCYON DAYS OF THE INTELLIGENT REANIMATED. BEFORE LONG, WE WILL BE WALKING THIS CONTINENT FROM COAST TO COAST, AND THEN IT WILL BE BUT A BOAT RIDE TO THE PRISTINE HUNTING GROUNDS OF EUROPE. SO MUCH TO DO. AS OUR NUMBERS GROW INTO THE HUNDREDS, THEN THOUSANDS, THEN MILLIONS - WE WILL, AS IF WITH OUR THUMB AND FOREFINGER, EXTINGUISH HUMAN HOPE.